MY FAVORITE

MIRACLE STORIES

JOE L. WHEELER

Pacific Press®
Publishing Association

Nampa, Idaho | Oshawa, Ontario, Canada
www.pacificpress.com

ALSO BY JOE L. WHEELER

Abraham Lincoln: A Man of Faith and Courage
Abraham Lincoln Civil War Stories:
Heartwarming Stories About Our Most
Beloved President
Amelia, the Flying Squirrel and Other
Great Stories of God's Smallest Creatures
Best of Christmas in My Heart 1
Best of Christmas in My Heart 2
A Bluegrass Girl
Candle in the Forest and Other Christmas Stories
Children Love
Christmas in My Heart®, books 1–23
Christmas in My Heart Treasuries
Christmas in My Heart, audio books 1–6
Christmas in My Soul, gift books (3)
Dick, the Babysitting Bear and Other Great Wild
Animal Stories
Easter in My Heart
Everyday Heroes
Great Stories Remembered, I, II, III
Great Stories Remembered, audio books I–III
Great Stories Remembered Classic Books (12 books)
Heart to Heart Stories for Dads
Heart to Heart Stories for Moms
Heart to Heart Stories of Friendship
Heart to Heart Stories for Grandparents
Heart to Heart Stories of Love
Heart to Heart Stories for Sisters
Heart to Heart Stories for Teachers
A Mother's Face Is Her Child's First Heaven
My Favorite Angel Stories
Only God Can Make a Dad

Owney, the Post Offie Dog and Other Great Dog Stories
Remote Controlled
Saint Nicholas (a Thomas Nelson Christian
Encounter biography)
The Secrets of Creeping Desert and Other Mystery
Stories for Boys
Showdown and Other Sports Stories for Boys
Smoky, the Ugliest Cat in the World and Other Great
Cat Stories
Spot, the Dog That Broke the Rules and Other Great
Heroic Animal Stories
St. Nicholas: A Closer Look at Christmas (with Canon
James Rosenthal)
Stinky, the Skunk That Wouldn't Leave and Other
Strange and Wonderful Animal Stories
Soldier Stories
Sooty, the Green-Eyed Kitten and Other Great
Animal Stories
Stories of Angels
The Talleyman Ghost and Other Mystery Stories for Girls
Tawny, the Magnificent Jaguar and Other
Great Jungle Stories
Tears of Joy for Mothers
Time for a Story
Togo, the Sled Dog and Other Great Animal Stories of
the North
The Twelve Stories of Christmas
What's So Good About Tough Times?
Wildfie, the Red Stallion and Other Great Horse Stories
The Wings of God
Zane Gray's Impact on American Life and Letters

DEDICATION

Though I never met the man, what I've learned about him fascinates me—especially because of his ecumenical outlook on angel and miracle stories. I already used many of the stories he collected for *My Favorite Angel Stories* (Pacific Press®, 2013). A number of years ago, a fellow appreciator of memorable stories unearthed, as a special gift, a very rare old book titled *The Hand That Intervenes* (Review and Herald®, 1918). So it's almost a hundred years old. It is easily the greatest collection of true, biblically compatible angel and miracle stories I have found during my lifetime. What a prodigious piece of scholarship! What impressed me the most is that this editor and compiler chose stories having to do with men and women of *many Christian faiths*—I can only imagine the work that must have taken. I'm guessing *many* years. Without this heirloom of a book, it would have been much more difficult for me to put together these two books.

Thus, it gives me great joy to dedicate this collection of miracle stories to that dynamo of energy:

William Ambrose [W. A.] Spicer
(1865–1952)

Cover design by Gerald Lee Monks
Cover illustration by Marcus Mashburn
Inside design by Aaron Troia

Scripture quotations are from the King James Version
unless otherwise noted.

Scripture quotations marked NKJV are taken from
the New King James Version®. Copyright © 1982
by Thomas Nelson. Used by permission.
All rights reserved.

Scripture quotations marked NLT are taken from the
Holy Bible, New Living Translation, copyright ©
1996. Used by permission of Tyndale House Publishers
Inc., Wheaton, Illinois 60189. All rights reserved.

You can obtain additional copies of this book by calling
toll-free 1-800-765-6955 or by visiting
http://www.adventistbookcenter.com.

www.joewheelerbooks.com

Representing the author is WordServe Literary Group
Ltd., 10152 Knoll Circle, Highland Ranch, CO 80130.

Library of Congress Cataloging-in-Publication Data

My favorite miracle stories / edited by Joe L. Wheeler.
    pages cm
  ISBN 13: 978-0-8163-5619-5 (pbk.)
  ISBN 10: 0-8163-5619-X
  1. Miracles. 2. Providence and government of
God—Christianity. 3. Coincidence—Religious aspects—
Christianity. I. Wheeler, Joe L., 1936- editor.
  BT97.3.M9 2015
  231.7'3—dc23
                                          2014040443

March 2015

CONTENTS

INTRODUCTION
Is There a Difference Between Miracle Stories and
Coincidence Stories?
Joseph Leininger Wheeler | 7
The Lord Spoke to Me
Dr. James Dobson | 11

SECTION ONE
The Boy in the Well
Mrs. Sam Woodson | 17
Prayer Heard and Answered
Author Unknown | 21
The Voice in the Tiger Jungle
Jacob Chamberlain | 23
The Unseen Hand
Jean Crager | 29
The Expunged Sermon
John F. Fletcher | 33
Poisoned in Tibet
William Carey | 37
A Box for Su Ling
Theresa Worman | 41
A Life-Changing Day on Humboldt Bay
Kirby Palmer, Connie Palmer Wheeler,
Marla Palmer Marsh | 47

SECTION TWO
His Daily Bread
Mrs. Howard Taylor | 53
A Raven the Messenger
S. W. Duffield | 57
Miracle in the Landhouse
A Narrative of Reformation Times | 61
Why the Horse Balked
Retold by H. W. Hastings | 65
Saved by a Spider's Web
Baxendale | 69

SECTION THREE
Snatched From the Green River
Byron Palmer | 73
A Rescue at Sea
Helen A. Steinhauer | 81
Oranges From Heaven
Miriam Kershaw | 85
Adrift in the Heavens
Myrtle Cossentine | 89
The Plane Engine That Wouldn't Start
Gary Marsh | 93
Jungle Landing
George Alden Thompson | 97
Miracle in Magdeburg
Paul K. Freiwirth | 103
Revolution!
Joseph Leininger Wheeler | 107

SECTION FOUR

An Angry Mob Held Powerless
Adam Clarke | 113

How Wang Was Called Into the Light
Hudson Taylor | 117

The Missionary Digs a Well
John G. Paton | 121

Protected
Mary Markham | 129

The Shadow
Jean Wingate | 137

Nondis the Leper
Marjorie Lewis Lloyd | 141

Another Chance
Dawn Boylan | 143

The Lighted Path
Mrs. R. B. Sheffer | 147

SECTION FIVE

He Shall Give His Angels Charge
Leta Walker | 153

Danger in the Dark
Louis W. Pettis | 157

Angels in the Fog
Lois Foreman | 161

Miracle on Highway 88
Steve Hamilton | 165

When Thou Walkest Through the Fire
Everett Smith | 169

My Prayer of Relinquishment
Teresa Sales | 173

The Girl Who Changed Her Mind
Margaret Eggleston | 177

God's Got Your Number!
Ken Gaub | 181

EPILOGUE

Miracle in the Sky
Joseph Leininger Wheeler | 185

Acknowledgments | 188

INTRODUCTION

IS THERE A DIFFERENCE BETWEEN MIRACLE STORIES AND COINCIDENCE STORIES?

Well, there certainly *ought* to be a difference. However, deciding which is which, for a story anthologist such as me, can sometimes be more than a little difficult.

Merriam-Webster helps some. "Miracle: An extraordinary event manifesting divine intervention in human affairs."

The catch, of course, is this: just how do we differentiate between divine intervention and mere coincidence? A crucial question, because many so-called miracle stories, upon close analysis, turn out to be merely a sequence of events that could be perceived as coincidental or the result of random throws of cosmic dice. Because of this, I have wrestled mightily with stories that, though they appear to be miraculous, turn out to be secular, devoid of any direct relationship to God. Which brings me to this conclusion: if there is no clear indication of divine intervention or involvement in a given story, I see no valid reason to consider it spiritually miraculous.

Without question, however, this conclusion has made my selection process extremely difficult, for many of the candidates for inclusion, even those that are overtly spiritual, border on the coincidental. Even a number that have been included in books printed by Christian publishing houses.

In the end, I've fallen back on the bedrock upon which I live and write: prayer. Every step of the way, when deciding whether or not to include a given story, I ask God to help me choose the right one. Because of this, certain stories I've decided to include gnaw at me both day and night, so that in order to get inner relief, I end up pulling them. And on the other hand, the same inner nagging takes place when I decide to leave out certain stories: I get no peace until I bring them back in. I've discovered multiple times that it is impossible to long resist divine nagging.

Are These Stories Sectarian?

Definitely not! Since our Lord, while on earth, never excluded anyone, neither should we. Christ set the bar in that respect, in what biblical scholars call the *Didache*. When a certain Pharisee tried to back Christ into a corner by asking Him which commandment was the most important of all, Christ answered in simple words that even two thousand years later, most Christians still attempt to live by:

> *"You must love the LORD your God with all your heart, all your soul, and all your mind." This is the first and greatest commandment. A second is equally important: "Love your neighbor as yourself." All the other commandments and all the demands of the prophets are based on these two commandments* (Matthew 22:37–40, NLT).

Consequently, I seek out biblically compatible stories that have to do with the direct relationship between God and each of His children, young or old. You will note that few of these stories identify the character in terms of religion. And the few that do are scattered through Christendom. For further exploration of this emphasis, read my dedication. ❧

Coda

I would love to hear from you, as to your reaction to these stories. You may even be able to track down authors to old stories or even descendants to those authors. You may reach me at:

Joe L. Wheeler, PhD
P.O. Box 1246
Conifer, CO 80433

I never cease to be amazed by God's incredible timing and choreography. The final galley edits for this book were due on November 14, 2014.

On Wednesday afternoon, November 12, completely out of the blue, I received one of my all-too-infrequent personal telephone calls from my cherished friend, Dr. James Dobson, legendary founder of both Focus on the Family and Family Talk.

In the course of our long chat, he thanked me for the copy of Christmas in My Heart 23 *I had sent him earlier; that led to my telling him about the next book,* My Favorite Miracle Stories, *which I was in the midst of my final galley edits for. He responded, "Have I sent you a copy of my new book?" "No," I answered, "shame on you!" He laughed and said, "I'll rush a copy off to you today."*

But the subject of miracles made him reflective: "Joe, let me tell you a story that's in my new book [Your Legacy]. *Do you have time for me to tell it to you?" "Of course!" I answered. Then he told me the story in its entirety, at times becoming emotional. Clearly he considered the story to be pivotal in his own life and ministry. At the end, after a long silence, I asked if he might possibly permit me to include it in my miracle book. "Of course!" was his response.*

Two days later, on November 14, FedEx delivered the book, personally inscribed, at the end of which was this postscript: "See pages 171–175."

As I look at the timing of those two days, I can reach no other conclusion but this: God willed that it anchor this collection of miracle stories.

The greatest endowment for your children and grandchildren can't be deposited in a bank. It can't be sold or traded or borrowed. It is an unshakable heritage of faith. It is the only gift that will stand the test of time. Everything else will fade away. Only by introducing your sons and daughters to Jesus Christ will you help them secure eternal life. How is that accomplished? By starting early and being intentional about the spiritual training of your children. It won't happen if left to chance. As we have seen, you also need to pray "without ceasing" for those you love (1 Thess. 5:17, NKJV). . . .

I said it before but it bears repeating. Modeling is the best evangelistic tool you have as young mothers and fathers. You might not have lived long enough to know that little boys and girls are watching your every move. In time, they will comprehend what matters most to you and what, deep inside, you don't actually care about. Your mannerisms and your quirks and your anger and your pleasures and your language and your "toys" will be incorporated into their own way of thinking. What you say is important, but what you *do* is infinitely more powerful. If you say that Jesus is Lord of your life, but you don't have time for devotions as a family while you are playing golf four hours every weekend, the contradiction will be observed.

I'll return to my godly father to illustrate how he transferred his beliefs to me. Through most of my childhood, he was an evangelist. He was not a perfect man, certainly, and he wasn't even at home much of the time. He traveled four to six weeks on each trip, leaving behind a wife he loved and needed—because he knew I needed her more. I can't describe fully the cost of that sacrifice for him. Nevertheless, when my father returned, he was ours, and some of my happiest days were spent hunting and fishing and playing tennis and building things with my six-foot-four dad.

Even so, this man's greatest contribution to my life was not represented by what he did for or with me; rather, it was the consistency of his Christian testimony. It made the most significant impact on me! He attempted to bring every area of his being into harmony with the Scriptures he loved so dearly. There in his home where faults and frailties were impossible to hide, I never once saw him deliberately compromise the principles in which he believed. Jesus Christ meant more to him than life itself.

We've been talking about money. Here is

how Dad felt about it. During the wartime years when everything was in short supply, he would drive hundreds of miles in an old car to visit a church that had called him to preach. They were usually small congregations, especially in the early years. Travel expenses were high and the "offering" given to evangelists was usually pitiful. In order to reduce costs, he typically stayed in pastors' homes during ten-day meetings. It was difficult, but being there gave him a firsthand look at the financial needs of the ministers and their families. More than once I remember my dad coming home after such a trip to greet my mother and me with warm embraces. Sooner or later, Mom would get around to asking the big question: "How much did they pay you?"

He would smile sheepishly and say, "Well . . . uh."

She then said, "I know. You gave it away again, didn't you?"

Dad would reply, "Yeah, Honey, I felt like I should. You know, that pastor has four kids and their shoes have holes in them. The oldest daughter doesn't even have a winter coat to wear to school, and I just couldn't leave there without helping them out. So I raised a 'love offering' for the pastor's family on the final Sunday night and contributed my check back to them."

Mom knew what that meant: Bills would come due without the money to pay for them. Yet to her credit, she would always smile and say, "If that's what God asked you to do, then you know it's OK with me."

Then the inevitable would happen. A few days later, our money would be exhausted. I can still recall Dad asking Mom and me to join him in the bedroom where we knelt in prayer. He always prayed first.

"Dear Lord, we come to You today with a small problem that You already know about. It concerns our shortage of money. You told us if we would be faithful to You in our good times, then You would stand by us in our hour of difficulty. We have tried to obey You and to share our resources with others; now my little family is the one in need. We ask You to help us especially at this time."

I was only nine years old, but I was listening carefully to what my father said to God in those moments. You can also be assured that I was waiting to see what the Lord would do in response, and I was never disappointed. I tell you truthfully that money always came from unexpected sources in time to meet our need. On one occasion that is still vivid in my memory, a $1,200 check arrived in the mail the day after our humble family prayer. My faith grew by leaps and bounds as I watched my parents practicing the scriptural principles on which their very lives were founded.

It is also true that my mother and father were not able to accumulate a nest egg during their working years, and I was concerned about them as they grew older. I worried about how they would pay for medical expenses and related obligations in their retirement years. I think my mother was worried about that, too. Women do tend to fret about things like that.

One day long after I was a man, my parents were scheduled to go out to dinner with friends. As usual, Dad got ready first. He was lying on the bed while Mom combed her hair. As she turned to look at him she noticed that he had tears in his eyes.

"What's the matter?" she asked.

He hesitated and then said, "The Lord just spoke to me."

"Do you want to tell me about it?" she asked.

"He told me something about you," said my father.

"Then you'd better tell me!" insisted Mom.

"Well, I was just lying here thinking," he said. "I wasn't even praying, but the Lord promised me that He was going to take care of you."

They wondered what the strange revelation could have meant and then went on with their evening plans. In my final telephone conversation with my dad, he told me this story. Five days later, my father suffered a massive heart attack from which he never recovered.

Being an only son, I was responsible for my mother's financial affairs after my dad's passing. I was alarmed to see that after the sale of her house and redeeming a couple of small life insurance policies, she only had $46,000 to take with her into the future. The church denomination in which my father had served for forty-two years offered almost nothing in the way of retirement benefit for its older ministers. The church had millions of dollars in its preachers' benevolent fund, but the leadership provided my mother with a paltry $58 per month—barely enough to keep gasoline in her car. Other men who pastored small churches that couldn't even make Social Security payments were hard-pressed to survive. It was disgraceful. If I hadn't been able to help provide for Mom financially, she could have been stuck in county facilities for the rest of her life.

Six years passed, and Mom contracted Parkinson's disease. She was hospitalized permanently. Her condition worsened and she required more and more care, eventually needing skilled nursing supervision twenty-four hours a day. Even in the late 1980s, the expense was in excess of $50,000 per year. Here's the miraculous part of the story: Right on schedule, the value of the stock Dad had inherited from his father almost fifty years earlier began to rise in value. Mom lived five more years before dying in 1988, and would you believe it, I never gave her a cent, because she didn't need it. He took care of Myrtle Dobson until the day she passed away. . . .

I had watched the life and times of my parents as the years unfolded through my young eyes. The faith that I learned at their knees is still vibrant, and it lives today within the hearts and minds of our grown children. God is faithful! And He keeps His word. ✣

SECTION ONE

"But soon a fierce storm arose. High waves began to break into the boat until it was nearly full of water. Jesus was sleeping at the back of the boat with his head on a cushion. Frantically they woke him up, shouting, 'Teacher, don't you even care that we are going to drown?' When he woke up, he rebuked the wind and said to the water, 'Quiet down!' Suddenly the wind stopped, and there was a great calm."
Mark 4:37–39 (NLT)

A little boy, Benny Hooper, had fallen into a well, and none of the efforts to extricate him alive worked. It all seemed hopeless.

But fifteen miles away, an inner voice was speaking to Sam Woodson.

How many of us, I wonder, would risk our lives for someone we'd never heard of before? Wouldn't we just reason, Surely somebody else will step in?

THE BOY IN THE WELL

Mrs. Sam Woodson

When I said goodbye to my husband, Sam, early that morning, we had no idea of the drama that was to engulf us before nightfall.

Sam left, and was on his way to work when he heard the news on the car radio. A little boy, Benny Hooper, had fallen down a well in his backyard over in Manorville, Long Island, just fifteen miles from our home. The desperate attempts of many people to get the boy out seemed to be failing.

Sam had a feeling then that he should go there and try to help. At work, he told the men in his carpool: "It's like God was saying 'Sam, you got to go to save that little boy.' " By 4:00 in the afternoon, Sam had even convinced his fellow workers. He got one of the men to drive him home, and I met him at the door.

"I'm going to Manorville," he said.

"Why? Why should you go?"

"I can't tell you exactly. It's just that I feel that I must. Once, in Virginia, I pulled a girl out of a forty-foot well. Maybe I can help in Manorville."

Then as he said goodbye to me, I told him to be careful and added, "I'll be at church all the while, Sam, praying for you and for the boy."

I knew that would mean a lot to Sam. He and I had been going to the Baptist church in Riverhead for twenty years. Sam sang bass in the gospel quartet there. I knew he would think the best thing I could do was to go to the church and pray for him and for the little boy.

So at 5:00 in the afternoon, twenty hours after the accident, Sam arrived at the Hoopers' backyard. The rescue was in full swing. Sam was just another of the six hundred people milling around the well and a big pit dug next to it.

Why should I be here? Sam began wondering to himself. *What makes me think I can even get near the well?* And sure enough, when he tried to work his way through the crowd, the police stopped him.

"I've got to go down," said Sam. He spied his boss, Michael Stiriz, who is a contractor in Long Island. Sam had heard that Mr. Stiriz had taken charge of the rescue.

"I want to go down, Mr. Stiriz," Sam shouted. Mr. Stiriz nodded, and the police let Sam through.

Sam saw the plan of rescue. It was too dangerous to dig right at the well itself. The walls might cave in. Mr. Stiriz had brought one of his big clam-bucket shovels and had dug another pit, shaped like a cone, twenty feet wide and narrow at the bottom, right next to Benny's prison. The pit was twenty-one feet deep, exactly the depth of the well. The distance was twelve feet, but because of the sandy soil and awkward position, only half the distance had been tunneled in twenty hours.

"What can I do?" Mr. Stiriz asked.

Sam looked at the dark tunnel angling off from the bottom of the pit. "Let's go," he said.

While I was praying in the church, Sam, too, got down on his knees, for a moment—and then slid into the tunnel on his stomach. The tunnel was made of a pipe, only twenty-seven inches in diameter. The air was hot and stuffy, and ahead was a wall of fine, saltlike, treacherous sand.

Sam came to the head of the tunnel, and began scraping the sand with his bare hands. As he worked, men in the pit behind him inched the pipe farther along with great construction jacks.

There was not enough oxygen in the pipe. Immediately Sam grew weak and dizzy, and felt the first of the cramps. They hit his shoulder. "Make the cramps go away, God," Sam said. He rested for a moment. They went away.

After an hour, Sam had made only a few inches of progress. The big trouble was big cave-ins at the head of the pipe. Sam was tired and sick to his stomach. He came out for a breather. One of the men up on the lip of the pit offered to take his place. The man did come down, but he took one look into the narrow tunnel and then climbed back up the ladder, shaking his head.

"Guess I've got to go back in," Sam said, and once again he got down on his knees and crawled forward toward the wall of sand separating him from the little boy he had never seen.

Sam dug on. The cramps came again, and he rested for a moment, talking all the while with God.

The second hour passed. Two hours of slow, painful scraping. Up above they were saying that Benny was dead. The doctor guessed there was only one chance in five that the boy was alive, yet Sam and all the others worked as hard as if the odds were reversed.

At 7:00 P.M., Sam came out for another breather; he had been down for two and a half hours! He could sense the tension growing up above. People knew something was about to happen. A hush fell over the crowd. Sam could hear a loudspeaker telling people not to smoke because they were afraid of causing an oxygen explosion. Ten tanks of oxygen had already been piped down the well to Benny. While he was taking the breather, Sam saw a red-eyed, haggard man peer over the pit's edge and then turn away.

"That's Benny's father," Mr. Stiriz said. "He hasn't slept all night, or all day either."

"Have you?" asked Sam.

Mr. Stiriz smiled. "No," he said. "No, I guess I haven't. Let's go."

Once again Sam inched his way along the narrow piping to the head of the tunnel. Behind him was another man, John Remick, who passed the sand back out of the pipe. Sam scratched away at the powdery sand, delicately, trying to keep it from caving in anymore.

Suddenly he felt his hand plunge forward. He paused a moment to make sure, then whispered back, "I've got through the well."

Mr. Remick passed the word along. Sam heard a sound like a moan pass through the crowd above. Very, very carefully now he scratched at the sand. He found little Benny's hand. It was cold.

"I think he's dead," Sam said.

Then there was another cave-in. Sam's arms and shoulders were covered. John Remick had to tug with all his force at Sam's heels to get him free.

Sam backed out of the cave-in sand and began the slow process of digging all over again. As the opening into the well shaft enlarged, Sam worked the sand from around the little red jacket that Benny had been wearing. It was resting on top of Benny's head. Sam saw that, miraculously, the life-giving oxygen hose had wormed its way through the folds of the jacket no more than an inch away from the boy's nose.

"Mmmmm. Ummmm . . ."

"Thank You, God. Thank You." Sam began to cry as he passed the word along. "The boy's alive."

Very slowly, very slowly now, Sam flicked away the sand from around Benny's body. Carefully he eased him out, up, and away from the well into the tunnel. Once a ray of light fell on Benny's eyes. The boy's eyes opened and he smiled at Sam.

"You still have your baby teeth, don't you?" Sam said. He talked again soothingly: "You come on easy now, Benny, it's going to be all right. All right." He inched the boy onto his shoulder.

"Don't move, now, just let me take you out slowlike." And Sam nestled little Benny Hooper onto his shoulder like he were the boy's brother.

At 7:40 P.M., three hours after Sam first went into the tunnel, he and John Remick climbed up the ladder carrying little Benny with them. The crowd was silent at first. Then suddenly it burst into a great cheering and crying, and an open, happy thanksgiving.

Hours later, Sam came home. There were visitors and people from the press, and people from the radio stations. But finally we were by ourselves.

"Do you remember when you asked me why should I go to Manorville?" Sam asked. "Well, I know now."

And then Sam reminded me that Benny had fallen into that well on May 17, and that May 17 was the date of the prayer crusade of my people down in Washington. He had even prayed that the Lord would let him go, because he wanted to be a part of a big, organized crusade for brotherhood.

But, somehow, Sam felt the Lord hadn't wanted him to go. So he stayed home, and kept wondering why the Lord hadn't wanted him to go. He wondered, that is, until he brought little Benny Hooper to the top of the rescue pit. At that moment a stranger came over to Sam and grasped his hand.

"Do you know," he said, "that you've done as much for brotherhood in three hours as most people could do in three lifetimes?"

Sam smiled. Now he knew why he had been called to Manorville. ❧

*T*hough she was alone and knew the end was near for her, she was convicted that she should send her daughter to aid old Mr. and Mrs. W. with food. And—sort of an afterthought—something else.

Again and again I've discovered, in studying true angel and miracle stories, that we serve a God who honors sincere prayer requests for "small things" just as much as He would were the request about a life-or-death matter.

One winter morning a Christian woman, who had often given food and clothing to the needy, sat alone in her room, where advanced age, and the beginning of what proved to be her last illness, confined her. Roused from her meditation by the entrance of her daughter, she said, "My dear, old Mr. and Mrs. W. have been on my mind all night. I hear that they are poor; they may be sick and in want. I wish you would take a basket, go to the city and buy a good supply of provisions, and take it to them." Here she gave the address, and as her daughter was leaving the room, she said, handing her a thick flannel skirt, "Perhaps you would do well to take this too; the weather is cold, and Mrs. W. may need it."

The young lady went. The provisions were bought, and at the head of the third flight of stairs in the tenement house to which she had been directed, she stopped. Through the door she heard Mr. W.'s voice asking a blessing upon the food before him. At the conclusion of the grace, and smiling at what she believed to be her mother's unnecessary anxiety, she knocked and entered. Sure enough, there they were at dinner, the wife at the foot of the table, waiting to be helped, the husband at the head, carving—one large apple, all the food they had!

With tears in her eyes, the daughter drew forth her kindly stores, and while a comfortable meal was being prepared, she listened to their grateful thanks, and heard from uncomplaining lips their pitiful story, of how they had fallen ill and had not been able to work, and so had been left destitute; how they had poured forth to God all their troubles, and how they believed that He would send someone to them. When dinner was ready and the visitor was about to leave, Mrs. W. accompanied her to the door, and with an expectant look, said, "My dear, did you bring the flannel skirt?"

In the excitement of her entrance, the daughter had quite forgotten the skirt that lay in the bottom of the basket. Astonished at the question, she said, "Yes, I brought you a skirt, but why do you ask?"

"Because, dear," said Mrs. W., "when I told the Lord there was only one apple left, I also told Him I needed a warm flannel skirt, and I was only wondering whether you had it, or if God would send it by someone else." ❧

It appeared that this would be the missionary's last night on earth; same for his porters. Only a miracle could save them.

I, too, have dialogued one on one with God and know how irresistible God is when for the third time He demands compliance, such as was true with Dr. Chamberlain in this story.

THE VOICE IN THE TIGER JUNGLE

Jacob Chamberlain

*"Thine ears shall hear a word behind
thee, saying, This is the way,
walk ye in it" (Isaiah 30:21).*

When the monsoon rains have raised the rivers of India over the banks, travel along the low country is attended with difficulty. Back in the mid-nineteenth century, there were still fewer facilities in the way of roads and river craft. About that time, Dr. Jacob Chamberlain was pioneering in the Godaveri District.

At a point where they expected to find a government steamer, they learned that the boat had broken down in battling against the fierce current. Their only course was to make a seventy-five-mile journey through the jungle. The first group coolie carriers deserted, followed by the armed guard.

Then the party met some hunters, and asked about the state of a stream two miles ahead, which they were hoping to cross in order to reach higher ground. "Impassable," the hunters said. The Godaveri was thirty feet above normal, and this branch was absolutely unfordable.

" 'Is there no boat?'

" 'None.'

" 'No material for a raft?'

" 'None whatever.'

"And on the hunters dashed for safety."

The doctor to his men, " 'If we press on to this little river, can we not make a raft of some kind and get over before dark?'

" 'Alas! There are no dry trees,' they said; 'and these green jungle trees will sink of themselves in the water, even if there were time to fell them.'

" 'Is there no knoll on this side that we can pitch on?'

" 'No; from river to bluff it is all like this.' We were standing in wet and mud as we talked.

" 'Keep marching on; I will consider what to do.' "

Then, as Dr. Chamberlain says in his book, *In the Tiger Jungle,* he drew back and rode behind the marching column in order to be more alone with God. Darkness would soon be upon them. He continues the story:

"Already we could hear the occasional fierce, hungry roar of the tigers in the rattan jungle at our right. I said not a word to my assistants, but I spoke to God. As my horse tramped on in the marshy path, my heart went up and claimed the promised presence.

" 'Master, was it not for Thy sake that we came here? Did we not covenant with Thee for the journey through? Have we not faithfully preached Thy name the whole long way? Have we shirked any danger, have we quailed before any foe? Didst Thou not promise, "I will be with thee"? Now we need Thee; we are in blackest danger for this night. Only Thou canst save us from this jungle, these tigers, this flood. O Master! Master! show me what to do!'

"An answer came, not audible, but distinct as though spoken in my ear by human voice: *Turn to the left, to the Godaveri, and you will find rescue.*

"Riding rapidly forward, I overtook the guides.

" 'How far is it to the Godaveri?'

" 'A good mile.'

" 'Is there no village on its banks?'

" 'No, none within many miles, and the banks are all overflowed.'

" 'Is there no mound, no rising ground, on which we could camp, out of this water?'

" 'It is all low and flat like this.'

"I drew apart and prayed again as we still plodded on. Again came the answer, *Turn to the left, to the Godaveri, and you will find rescue.*

"Again I called to the guides and questioned them: 'Are you sure there is no rising ground by the river where we can pitch, with the river on one side for protection and campfires around us on the other, through the night?'

" 'None whatever.'

" 'Think well; is there no dry timber of which we could make a raft?'

" 'If there were any, it would all be washed away by these floods.'

" 'Is there no boat of any sort on the river? I have authority to seize anything I need.'

" 'None nearer than the cataract.'

" 'How long would it take us to reach the Godaveri by the nearest path?'

" 'Half an hour; but it would be so much time lost, for we would have to come back here again, and cut our way through this jungle to the bluff, and climb that; there is no other way of getting around these two flooded streams that we must pass to reach the cataract.'

" 'How long would it take us to cut our way through to the bluff?'

" 'At least six hours; it will be dark in about an hour.'

" 'What shall we do for tonight?'

" 'God knows.' And they looked the despair they felt.

"I drew aside again and prayed as I rode on. *Turn to the left, to the Godaveri, and you will find rescue,* came the response the third time. It was not audible; none of those near heard it. I cannot explain it, but to me it was as distinct as though spoken by a voice in my ear; it thrilled me. 'God's answer to my prayer,' said I, 'I cannot doubt. I must act, and that instantly.'

"Hastening forward to the guides at the head of the column, 'Halt!' said I, in a voice to be heard by all. 'Turn sharp to the left. Guides, show us the shortest way to the Godaveri. Quick!'

"They remonstrated stoutly that it was only labor lost, that we should be in a worse plight there than here, for the river might rise higher and wash us away in the darkness of the night.

" 'Obey!' said I. 'March sharp, or night will come. I am master here, and intend to be obeyed. Show the way to the river.'

"They glanced at the fourteen-inch revolver that I held in my hand, ready for any beast that should spring upon us. They suspected that it might be used on something besides a beast, and one saying to the other, 'Come on, we've got to go,' started on.

"All the party had surrounded me. My native preachers looked up inquiringly at my awed face. 'There is rescue at the river,' was all I said. How could I say more?

"Providentially we had just come to where an old path led at right angles to our former course and directly toward the river, and down that path we went. The step of all was quicker than before.

" 'The *dhora* has heard of some help at the river,' I overheard the coolies say to one another. I had heard of help, but what it was I knew not. My anxiety seemed to have gone; there was an intense state of expectancy in its place. Half a mile from the river I spurred forward past the guides; I knew the coolies would not desert me now. There was no place of safety they could reach for the night; they would cling around me for protection.

"I cantered out from among the bushes to the bank, keenly observant. There, right under my feet, was a large flatboat tied to a tree at the shore, with two men upon it trying to keep it afloat in the rising and falling current.

" 'How did this boat get here?' said I.

" 'Oh, sir, please don't be angry with us,' said one of the boatmen, taking me to be an officer of the British India government, to whom the boat belonged, and thinking I was taking them to task for not keeping the boat at its proper station. 'We tried our best to keep the boat from coming here, but, sir, it seemed as though it was possessed. This morning we were on our station on the upper river, caring for the boat as usual, when a huge rolling wave came rushing down the river, and snapped the cables, and swept the boat into the current. We did our utmost to get it back to that bank of the river, but it would go farther and farther out into the current. The more we pulled for the British bank the more it would work out toward the Nizam's. We have fought all day to keep it from coming here, but it seemed as though a supernatural power was shoving the boat over, and an hour ago we gave up, and let it float in here, and tied it up for safety to this tree. Don't be angry, sir; as soon as the river goes down or gets smooth, we will get the boat back where it belongs. Don't have us punished for letting it come here; we could not help it.'

" 'All right, my men,' said I. 'I take command of this boat. I have authority to use any government property I require on this journey. I shall use the boat, and reward you well, and give you a letter to your superior that will clear you of all blame.'

"The boat, a large flatboat with strong railings along both sides, and square ends to run upon the shore, had been built by the British military authorities in the troublous times following the mutiny in those regions, and placed on an affluent of the Godaveri, higher up on the north bank, to ferry artillery and elephants across in their punitive expeditions, and it was still kept there. These men were paid monthly wages to keep it always ready at its station, in case of sudden need.

"Who had ordered that tidal wave in the morning of that day, that had torn the boat from its moorings and driven it so many miles down the river; that had thwarted every endeavor of the frightened boatmen to force it to the north shore, and had brought it to the little covelike recess just where we would strike the river? Who but He on whose orders we had come; He who had said, 'I will be with you'; He who knew beforehand the dire straits in which we would be in that very place, on that very day, that very hour; He who had told us so distinctly, *Turn to the left, to the Godaveri, and you will find rescue*? I bowed my head, and in amazed reverence I thanked my God for this signal answer to our pleading prayer." ❧

*I*t was bitterly cold in the train that day high in the Andes Mountains. Snow on all sides of them, and the elevation (13,000, 14,000, 15,000 feet high) took one's breath away. But as if that wasn't more than enough, suddenly there was a terrible jolt—the train was off the track!

In this train high in the Andes were Protestants, Catholics, and unbelievers, each of whom trembled at the imminence of death. We assume God would be more likely to answer a Christian's prayer; but, not being divine, we don't know for sure. What if it were an unbeliever's first prayer in all of his life that moved God most?

The Unseen Hand

Jean Crager

Mother, can't we eat yet?" begged seven-year-old Betty from the depths of a big blanket in which she was snugly wrapped and tucked on the seat.

"Why, it's only ten o'clock. Surely my little girl isn't hungry again, so soon after a big breakfast." This from Daddy as he consulted his watch.

And to settle the matter beyond a doubt, Mother said, "We had better wait until twelve o'clock. Don't you think so?"

Daddy and Mother, sister, Betty, and baby had been riding on the little mountain train since early morning, and had found its wooden benches very hard and its unheated coaches very cold. An attempt had been made to heat the cars, but it had been an utter failure, resulting in so much smoke that all the windows had to be raised to save the passengers from asphyxiation, and the air that rushed into the car, sweeping down from the peaks of the Andes Mountains, was none too warm. Therefore, it was not strange that all who had blankets or other warm covering at hand used them to good advantage to keep stiff fingers and toes from completely freezing.

"Daddy, why does that lady over there wear black glasses and the old man with white hair wear green ones?" The little girl was at her game of asking questions again.

"Look out of the window at the white snow," said Daddy. "Now tell me what the white snow does to your eyes if you look at it a long time when the sun shines on it."

"I know why, Daddy," exclaimed sister, who had been listening to Betty's and Daddy's conversation. "It's because the white snow makes people's eyes hurt after a while."

To Betty's delight, Daddy let her look through *his* sunglasses, and everything greatly surprised her by looking very dull. "Oh, everything looks so dark. I wouldn't like to wear these all the time," she decided.

Just then a sandwich boy came through the train. His appearance reminded the hungry little girl of the lunch in the rack above her head; so "What time is it, Daddy?" popped into her busy little brain, and she said it. To her great satisfaction it was noon, and the lunch was thoroughly enjoyed. Then Mother told her little girls some stories, and they watched from the window as the train climbed the mountain sides, wound around bends and through tunnels, and finally ran between high walls of snow left on each side by the snowplow when it cleared the track. During the afternoon they stopped at a little station way up on top of the Andes, and Daddy took the girls to the shed where the big snowplow was kept, and showed them how it worked. As the winter season was just over, it had worked hard for several weeks, opening up the road so that this, the first train attempting the trip since winter, could cross. The men who worked on the steam shovel had driven their machine through drifts more than twelve feet high; so several times during the day nothing could be seen on either side but banks of snow much higher than the train itself.

At the little station, the passengers who were cold tried to warm themselves by doing exercises in the snow, but they were not long in finding out that at an altitude of between thirteen thousand and fifteen thousand feet above sea level the average person does not care to do strenuous walking or exercise of any kind. Many of the passengers suffered from mountain sickness during the day.

Toward evening Daddy began to feel quite relieved that the dangerous part of the journey had been completed, for three more hours would bring the little train to Los Andes, a town at the foot of the mountains on the Chilean side. Snow avalanches are a continual menace here during the early part of spring, because then the snow begins to thaw and sweeps down the mountainside, carrying everything with it to the valley below. When a snowslide does close the possibility of crossing by train, it is necessary to cross the pass on the backs of burros, those faithful little sure-footed creatures

who don't seem to mind the intense cold prevailing near the "Christ of the Andes," a statue which marks the boundary between Argentina and Chile.

And then, without a moment's warning, sister, who was asleep on one of the benches, was rudely bounced into the air; the children's pet canary was tossed against the side of his wire cage, and his little water dish emptied itself unceremoniously onto the bench where Betty was sitting. Mother held baby tight and gasped, "The train is off the track," and Daddy started from his seat just in time to stop a small bag in its descent from the baggage racks overhead. He told Mother to sit still and not get frightened, for they were doing God's work and He would take care of them.

The plump woman down at the other end of the car promptly fainted, but was duly revived with the aid of smelling salts and a dash of cold water.

By this time the two black-robed nuns across the aisle from Betty sensed that something was wrong, and began to say the "Ave Maria" and count the beads of their heavy rosaries, stopping occasionally to kiss the crucifix, which hung from the end of the beads.

Above the din and confusion rose the invocations to the virgin Mary, Saint Peter, and especially to Saint Antonio, Chile's patron saint and protector.

The stout old gentleman with the gray mustache stood up, walked to the other end of the coach, came back to his seat, and repeated the process numberless times during the few short minutes in which the car jolted over the ties and bed of the railroad. He seemed very nervous about a small package that he carried with him during this running back and forth, and which he seemed to prize highly. Perhaps it was a dozen eggs, or maybe a stick of dynamite that might explode any moment.

Providentially, no one but the engineer knew just where all this was taking place; for if, in the first moments, the passengers had realized that the train was nearing a high trestle bridge over the Rio Blanco and that the bridge was only wide enough for a single track, with barely a foot of extension on each side, many would probably have followed the example of one of the passengers. This man went out to the rear platform of the derailed coach and prepared to leap to his death more than two hundred feet below. At the last minute he lost his courage and was afraid. A few moments later, he reentered the car and informed his fellow passengers that theirs was the only derailed coach, and that the two cars behind and the two ahead might possibly keep it from turning over, though already the car leaned dangerously to one side. This man also told about the bridge they were approaching, which would mean positive destruction. If the car didn't tip over and drag the rest of the train with it, he declared, it would become uncoupled as soon as it struck the first open ties of the trestle bridge.

Now the rushing of the water could be heard above the confusion and noise. The brakes screeched and groaned as the brakeman attempted to stop the train. The engineer, thinking of the many lives depending on him, grew pale and fought grimly with the engine, which was racing toward the bridge. He *must* stop before they got there!

A second later, the engine had started across the bridge. There were still several yards to go before it would reach the open ties, which would spell death to the people in the derailed car. All the passengers were in a state of suspense. They now knew where they were and what it all meant. Any moment might be their last.

The engine reached the open ties and still the brakes had not brought the train to a standstill. Then the miracle happened! Just as the front wheels of the derailed coach came to the first open tie, an unseen hand stopped the train! Sighs of relief mingled with thanksgiving psalms to the saints, and cries of joy with prayers of gratitude to God.

As they got out of the car to await its replacing on the rails, Daddy took Betty's hand and showed her what would have happened if God had not stopped the train just in time. He pointed to the river below and said, "If God had not stopped that train and kept the car from tipping over, we would be down there now."

Now Betty is no longer a little girl. She is a student in college, preparing to do the work for which God spared her life that day; but she always thinks of that experience as a direct manifestation of the love and protection of her heavenly Father. How do I know what she thinks about it? Well, you see, I'm Betty! ❧

What worse thing could happen than to memorize your sermon, stand up to preach, and forget everything? Not even remembering the subject of the sermon!

THE EXPUNGED SERMON

John F. Fletcher

An associate of John Wesley, John F. Fletcher, was one of the eminent men of early Methodism. He related an experience, which is preserved in a "Life of Mr. Fletcher," included in the complete "Works" of Wesley.

On standing up to preach one Sunday at Madeley, John Fletcher had the entire topic upon which he had prepared to speak taken from his mind. Neither text nor subject matter could he recall. In his confusion and embarrassment, he had recourse to the morning Scripture lesson that he had just read, the third chapter of Daniel. He commented for a time on the lesson of the three Hebrew children and the fiery furnace. He says:

"I found in doing it such an extraordinary assistance from God, and such a peculiar enlargement of heart, that I supposed there must be some peculiar cause for it. I therefore desired, if any of the congregation found anything in particular, they would acquaint me with it in the ensuing week.

"In consequence of this, the Wednesday after, a woman came, and gave me the following account:

" 'I have been for some time much concerned about my soul. I have attended the church at all opportunities, and have spent much time in private prayer. At this my husband (who is a butcher) has been exceedingly enraged, and threatened me severely what he would do if I did not cease going to John Fletcher's church; yea, if I dared to go any more to any religious meeting whatsoever.

" 'When I told him I could not in conscience refrain from going at least to our parish church, he grew quite outrageous, and swore dreadfully, if I went any more, he would cut my throat as soon as I came home.

" 'This made me cry mightily to God, that He would support me in the trying hour; and though I did not feel any great degree of comfort, yet having a sure confidence in God, I determined to go on in my duty and leave the rest to Him.

" 'Last Sunday, after many struggles with the devil and my own heart, I came downstairs ready for church. My husband asked me whether I was resolved to go thither. I told him I was. "Well, then," said he, "I shall not (as I intended) cut your throat; but I will heat the oven and throw you into it the moment you come home."

" 'Notwithstanding this threatening, which he enforced with many bitter oaths, I went to church, praying all the way that God would strengthen me to suffer whatever might befall me. While you were speaking of the three children whom Nebuchadnezzar cast into the burning fiery furnace, I found it all had to do with me, and God applied every word to my heart.

" 'When the sermon was ended, I thought, *If I had a thousand lives I could lay them all down for God.* I felt my whole soul so filled with His love that I hastened home fully determined to give myself to whatsoever God pleased, nothing doubting but that either He would take me to heaven if He suffered me to be burned to death, or that He would some way deliver me, even as He did His three servants that trusted in Him.

" 'When I got almost to our own door, I saw the flames issuing out of the mouth of the oven, and I expected nothing else but that I should be thrown into it immediately. I felt my heart rejoice, that if it were so, the will of the Lord would be done. I opened the door, and to my utter astonishment saw my husband upon his knees, wrestling with God in prayer for the forgiveness of his sins. He caught me in his arms, earnestly begged my pardon, and has continued diligently to seek God ever since.' "

Mr. Fletcher added, "I now know why my sermon was taken from me; namely, that God might thus magnify His mercy" (*Works of John Wesley,* vol. 6, p. 465). ❧

The Tibetans had deliberately poisoned this early Christian missionary, then gathered to watch her die.

What should she do?

Even though you and I may read in Scripture that God will overrule natural laws when a Christian is poisoned and calls upon Him to honor that biblical promise, would our faith be strong as was Annie Taylor's—and really believe God would do it?

Among the pioneers in Tibetan work was Miss Annie Taylor, who died some years ago in England. With a burden on her soul for Tibet, she lived among the Tibetans on the Indian side of the border till she learned the language. Then, in 1890, she pushed over the frontier in spite of regulations—a young woman, and alone, taking her stand on the forbidden ground by authority of the gospel commission, "Go ye into all the world." Of her first experiences, famed Baptist missionary William Carey in his *Adventures in Tibet,* wrote:

> Her presence was obnoxious to the authorities, and she was ordered to leave the valley. The captain of the guard of the Dong-Kya Pass came over from the Chinese fort at Khamba-jong to settle what should be done. Finally she was moved to Tumlong, and given a room in the monastery there. But the people had been told not to sell her any food, so she found it difficult to live. On one occasion she followed a caravan over the stony roads, and eased her hunger a little by picking up the grains of parched corn which dribbled through a small hole in one of the packs carried by a mule.

Again, in emergencies, women would secretly drop their popped corn in the roadway, and "she would pick it up like the birds of the air, thanking God for the timely supply."

Still she held on for Christ and Tibet, refusing to be driven out. At last it was determined to kill her. The *Missionary Review* of April 1894 tells part of the story as follows:

> The natives would ask her frequently what they were to do with her body if she died. She told them she was not going to die just then. They have, however, a custom of "praying people dead," and to this they resorted, taking care to help their prayers in a very effective manner. One day the chief's wife invited the stranger to eat, and prepared rice and a mixture of eggs for her. Some conversation between the women as she was eating aroused Miss Taylor's suspicion as to the eggs placed before her, and, sure enough, after she had partaken she became ill, with all the symptoms of aconite poisoning.

How she escaped has perhaps never been put in print, as Miss Taylor said little publicly of the most intimate experiences with the Lord's delivering hand. But a personal friend of hers—one of the writer's acquaintances in London, now dead—told us that Miss Taylor believed that God interposed in a miraculous way to save her from death by the poison. She felt her strength going; her heart was ceasing to act; and as she looked out, she saw a crowd gathering silently about. She knew then that she had been poisoned by deliberate and deadly design, and that the people were gathering in curiosity to see her die.

There she was, a young woman all alone in dark Tibet; yet not alone, for there was One who has promised His messengers, "Lo, I am with you alway" [Matthew 28:20]. His angels were there, and His Spirit in that moment brought to her mind the promise, "If they drink any deadly thing, it shall not hurt them" [Mark 16:18]. The conviction came that God would save her, and with strength ebbing she laid hold of that promise, and asked God to verify it just then—not for her sake alone, but for Tibet's sake.

Immediately she felt the blood again tingling in her veins, her heart began working normally, her strength returned, and rising up in the strength of the Lord, she took her Tibetan Scripture portion and went out to preach Jesus and His power to save to those who had gathered to see her die. ❧

*L*ittle Su Ling, of the Hong Kong Christian Orphanage, had learned a lot about the God the missionaries served and worshiped. So much so that her faith in God's promises even surpassed that of the missionaries.

But not this time. They tried to prepare her for certain disappointment and loss of faith.

Would I have as much faith as Su Ling—or would I have temporized like the Christian missionaries? Really, I'm afraid to answer.

A Box for Su Ling

Theresa Worman

*A*nother Christmas in Hong Kong, thought Pat Mordell to himself as he walked down one of the narrow, dirty streets.

As Pat walked along, he saw a bundle of old rags up against one of the buildings. *I won't look,* thought Pat, *for if the bundle moves, I'm a goner.*

Pat had the softest heart when it came to boys and girls. Many times he had seen bundles of rags just like that one over by the building and inside of them was a half-starved Chinese boy or girl. Pat could never pass them by. He'd carry them to Miss Fraser at the Christian Orphanage.

Each time Pat brought such a bundle, Miss Fraser would say, "No more, Pat. Please don't bring us another child. There just isn't enough for one more mouth." And Pat would say, "OK. This will be the last one."

But in a few days, he would clang the bell at the orphanage and Miss Fraser would accept the bundle of rags with a boy or girl inside. And Pat would go away happy that another little child was going to be fed and loved.

Today Pat tried hard to look straight ahead and not glance at the bundle of rags, but he just couldn't help it. As he looked out of the corner of his eye, he saw a little face peer out of the rags.

Pat thought of his Timmy in the United States with more food than he could eat and Christmas toys galore. He looked down at this little Chinese girl dying in a bundle of rags right on the street. Pat glanced up to the sky, and a little song Timmy sang came to him:

Jesus loves the little children,
All the children of the world.
Red and yellow, black and white,
All are precious in His sight.
Jesus loves the little children of the world.

Pat walked over and picked up the bundle of rags in his big, strong arms. He walked with great long steps right up to the gate of the orphanage and gave the bell rope a yank.

Miss Fraser came to the door. "Pat," she said, "you promised there would be no more." All the time her heart was aching to take the little one in and love her and feed her.

"I know, Miss Fraser," said Pat, "but with Christmas coming on, I just couldn't leave her on the street to die, could I? I really won't be bringing any more children to you after today, Miss Fraser, because I'm sailing at noon."

"Oh, we'll miss you, Pat. The Lord bless you. It will be nice to get home to your Timmy, won't it? Too bad you can't make it by Christmas," said Miss Fraser, as she said goodbye to the big Marine she'd grown fond of.

Soft black eyes looked up in wonder as Miss Fraser's hands stroked the matted hair of the little one. She asked in the child's own language, "What is your name, little one?"

"Su Ling," answered a small voice from among the rags.

"We're going to take off these dirty clothes, Su Ling, and wash you and put some clean clothes on you. Won't that be nice? Then we're going to give you something good to eat, and tuck you into bed for a nap," said Miss Fraser.

Su Ling had never in her life had a bath like the one they gave her. When they put a flannelette nightgown on her, she thought it was the softest thing she had ever felt. Then she was fed good warm rice.

It is surprising what food and love can do for a little starved child. Su Ling had been at the orphanage only a few months when she accepted the Lord Jesus as her very own Savior. With the Lord Jesus making His home in her heart, a light shone on her face. The teachers and the children said, "Su Ling has the Jesus shine on her face." And it was true. Many of the children in the orphanage loved the Lord Jesus, but not one loved Him more than Su Ling.

For three years Su Ling lived in the orphanage, three wonderful, happy years. For three Christmases the kind people of Hong Kong and others from over the sea supplied her with things dear to a little girl's heart. The first Christmas she wanted only a place to sleep and food for her starved body, for Pat had brought her to the orphanage just six days before Christmas. But on Christmas morning a rag doll was tucked in bed beside her. How she loved the soft, cuddly doll! She never felt alone after the doll came to share her little cot. The second Christmas she had helped make the Christmas decorations and had recited a Christmas piece at the program. Now it was near the third Christmas. Miss Soong, one of the Chinese teachers, had said that Christmas was a time for giving gifts, because God had given His best Gift, His own Son, the Lord Jesus, on that first Christmas Day long ago. Su Ling wanted to give gifts this year, rather than to be the one to receive them.

Then Su Ling got a big, bold thought. She thought how wonderful it would be to give every girl and boy and every teacher in the orphanage a Christmas present. Now, remember, Su Ling was a little orphan girl with only two dresses, a doll, a few colored ribbons, a string of beads, and a New Testament. That is all she owned in the world besides five or six picture cards. And she had no way of earning money.

Imagine getting an idea to give Christmas gifts to all the children in the orphanage! Did you ever hear of anything like it?

She had thought about the Christmas presents before the American traveler came to talk to them, but it was he who showed her how to get her presents. The American traveler told of many wonderful things God had done for him in answer to prayer. Su Ling sat and listened to every word. She heard how in answer to prayer, money had been given to him for his trip, how he had lost his suitcases and trunks when a Chinese junk had sunk, but God, in answer to prayer, had supplied him with everything he needed, and even with some extra things. "God is your Father. If you want anything, just ask Him, believing He can do it, and He will." That's what the American traveler said, and Su Ling believed him.

"God can do anything, can't He, Miss Soong?" asked Su Ling one day.

"Indeed He can," said Miss Soong.

"Could He do something for a girl like me if I wasn't selfish and wanted the something for other people?" asked Su Ling.

"I'm sure He could," said Miss Soong.

"I've asked Him for some presents for Christmas," said Su Ling.

"That's nice," said Miss Soong. "I'm sure you'll get something nice." She wasn't paying very close attention.

"I've asked Him for two hundred and eighty-eight presents," continued Su Ling.

What? Miss Soong almost dropped the shirt she was stitching. "Two hundred and eighty-eight presents? What would you do with that many, Su Ling? That's kind of selfish, isn't it?"

"Oh, but I told you, they are not for me. You see, the first Christmas I was here I got all the rice I wanted and some sweets and a rag doll. And last Christmas I got a new dress, some candy, and a nice book. I don't want to be getting and getting and never giving. The man from America got lots of things by just asking God, so I decided that this Christmas I'm going to ask God to give me two hundred and eighty-eight presents for all the children in the orphanage and for the teachers and for old Chang, the gatekeeper."

"Oh, Su Ling, that's asking God for a lot!" exclaimed Miss Soong.

"But God can do it, can't He?" insisted Su Ling.

"Yes, but—but—" Miss Soong didn't know what to say. She'd have to talk to Miss Fraser.

Su Ling was in the sewing room the next day when Miss Fraser came in and sat down beside her.

"Su Ling, Miss Soong was telling me—" But she got no further, for Su Ling looked up with her eyes dancing. "Isn't it wonderful, Miss Fraser, that God can give me presents for the children? He owns everything in the world, and the American said, 'Whatsoever ye shall ask in prayer, believing, ye shall receive.' "

Miss Fraser, seeing Su Ling's simple faith in God her Father, didn't say what she had come to say.

The missionaries prayed much about Su Ling that Christmas. Some prayed, "O God, don't let her be too disappointed if the gifts do not come." One prayed, "O God, we know that Thou hast promised to supply our need, and we believe that Thou canst give these extra things to Su Ling, but we do not know how.

Work it out, O God, for we are baffled. There is nothing we can do."

The faith of the missionaries got weaker and weaker as Christmas drew near. But not Su Ling's faith. The closer Christmas came, the more certain she was that God was going to answer her prayer.

Christmas came nearer and nearer, and the children were bursting with excitement. Every boy was to have a new shirt; every girl was to have a new dress. There would be extra sweets and perhaps a toy for each of the younger children. Excitement ran high.

The only place where a bit of gloom crept in was in the room where the missionaries and the Chinese helpers met for prayer and to decide things concerning the work. They all felt bad because they had not figured out a way to help God answer Su Ling's prayer. They were afraid her heart would be broken on Christmas Day when her prayer was not answered.

The last boat from the United States before Christmas had come in with some boxes for the orphanage. One box, about eighteen or twenty inches long, wrapped in pretty Christmas paper, was for Su Ling. The True Blue Class had promised to send her a doll. "I'm sure it's a beautiful doll," said Miss Fraser. "The girls in that class send such lovely things. But I'm afraid a doll won't give her much pleasure when she's expecting two hundred and eighty-eight presents."

It was a sad group of missionaries and helpers who took their places among the children the day of the Christmas service.

The program was lovely, the nicest one that had ever been given. The smaller children had their parts first. They were darling as they sang their little song about the Baby Jesus lying in a manger. Then the primary and junior children acted out the Christmas story, and they did it very well. One of the Chinese teachers explained what Christmas means.

He said, "To God the Father, Christmas meant giving His Son. 'For God so loved the world, that he gave his only begotten Son, that whosoever believeth in him should not perish, but have everlasting life' [John 3:16].

"To God the Son, it meant leaving beautiful heaven to become an obedient servant, obedient even unto death. 'Christ Jesus . . . took upon him the form of a servant . . . and became obedient unto death, even the death of the cross' [Philippians 2:7].

"To the world, it meant that God had provided a Savior. For the angel said, 'I bring you good tidings of great joy, which shall be to all people. For unto you is born this day in the city of David a Saviour, which is Christ the Lord' [Luke 2:11].

"To you, it means that God gives you eternal life as a gift. 'For as many as received him [the Lord Jesus], to them gave he power to become the sons of God, even to them that believe on his name' [1 John 1:12]."

When the teacher finished giving the Christmas message, several of the children accepted the Lord Jesus as their Savior.

The time for giving out the gifts had come. Miss Fraser handed each child a present as they marched past the Christmas tree. Miss Soong gave each one a piece of candy. Dark eyes sparkled and white teeth flashed big smiles. There were tears in Miss Fraser's eyes as she handed the box from the True Blue Class to Su Ling. "Here's a pretty doll for you, Su Ling, from the True Blue Class in America." Su Ling thanked her, but glanced inquiringly at the few packages still under the tree. There was no doubt in her heart but that the gifts she had prayed for must be there.

Two big tears rolled down Miss Fraser's cheeks and fell *kerplunk* on the book she handed to the child in line after Su Ling. She decided they would have to teach the children not to pray for unnecessary things. They must realize that one had to be practical in what one asked God for. She didn't know how they'd do it, but they must never let this happen again.

Su Ling took her seat and looked at the pretty tag on her box. She broke the red ribbon very carefully, rolled it up, and put it in her pocket. She took the pretty Christmas paper off the package and folded it up, putting it in her pocket with the ribbon. Then she looked inside the box.

Oh, how pretty! she thought. Bowing her head for a moment, she said, "Dear Father, I thank You. I didn't know what to ask You for, that the children and the big people would like. I would never have thought of this gift, but You knew just what to send. Thank You, Father. Amen."

Su Ling quietly left her chair and went up to Miss Fraser and said, "Miss Fraser, may I give out my gifts now?"

"Your gifts? What do you mean, Su Ling? Wasn't there a doll in the box I gave you?" asked the astonished missionary.

"No, Miss Fraser. I don't need a doll; I have one. But look at all the pretty combs. I'm sure there are enough for all the children and the teachers and old Chang." Miss Fraser looked through her tears and saw combs of all colors: red, yellow, green, blue, pink.

Su Ling started at the front row and handed everyone in the place a nice little pocket comb. How thrilled they were! When old Chang got his, he combed his hair right there with some extra fancy motions that made all the children laugh.

All during the next year when the rice ran low and one might have become discouraged, someone would say, "Remember the combs." That would brighten up everyone, for they knew that the God who had sent 288 combs to Su Ling would in answer to believing prayer send rice for His children. ❧

*T*his particular story had been gestating in the minds of three siblings for sixty-five years. It has to do with a pivotal day that came so close to being their last that, even after all these years, it seems like it was only yesterday. So each of them wrote out the story. What follows is the synthesis of the three.

It would be more than a slight understatement for me to declare that this story means a great deal to me—for, if God had not intervened, I might never have had the opportunity to fall in love with and marry the Connie in this story.

A Life-Changing Day on Humboldt Bay

Kirby Palmer,
Connie Palmer Wheeler, Marla Palmer Marsh

It was the summer of '49, when it was decided to take a church group for an afternoon ride on a fishing boat. It was cloudy and windy as a multigenerational crowd of children, teenagers, young adults, and senior citizens climbed on board for what was expected to be a pleasant and serene ride on Humboldt Bay.

Aboard were a number of families, including the Palmers; the Tanners; Dr. and Mrs. Clarence Atteberry; and the legendary radio evangelist H. M. S. Richards and his wife and son, Harold M. S. Richards Jr. H. M. S. Richards, who founded the *Voice of Prophecy* radio broadcast, was then seeing tremendous growth in the program's reach: moving that year from the 608 radio stations on the Mutual Broadcasting Network to an even bigger venue on the ABC network. Harold Richards Jr. had been working all summer at the Pacific Lumber Company in Scotia to earn money for college, and his parents had driven up to the Fortuna area of Northern California to join the church group for this Fourth of July festivity.

Dolores Chester, an effervescent teenager from Eureka, had persuaded her father, who owned the fishing boat, to take this church group (of some thirty to thirty-five people) on the boat ride.

After cruising south towards Fields Landing, Mr. Chester turned his boat around and headed back toward port. But Dolores and the other young people were having such a grand time that they begged Mr. Chester to take them outside the protective jetty into the ocean a little ways before taking them back to the dock. But Mr. Chester didn't think that was a good idea at all, for the tide was changing, which would result in bigger and more dangerous wave action in the vicinity of the open channel.

But finally, bowing to the pressure of his daughter and the other young people, Mr. Chester caved in and agreed to take them through the open channel into the Pacific—but just a little ways.

As they approached the jetty, the waves got bigger and bigger; suddenly they were crashing over the bow and rushing alongside the captain's cabin, catching those in the rear of the vessel by surprise.

Simultaneously, there came over the radio an urgent message from the Coast Guard, whose headquarters loomed to the right: "Do you have the legally required life jackets for all your passengers?" To his chagrin, Mr. Chester had to admit he did not. He hadn't expected to take his boat beyond the jetty in the first place. The ride through to the jetty was not normally dangerous. With experienced fishermen on board there would have been little problem, but here he was, with a flat-decked boat, room enough in the captain's cabin for only two, with over thirty people on board—a number who didn't even know how to swim—and without life jackets! Other than the pipe railings on the boat, there was precious little for the passengers to hang on to: only two one-inch pipe railings that went along the edge of the boat for people to grasp.

Now, as the boat descended each wave to the bottom of the trough and hit the face of the next wave, the boat appeared to dig in and shudder at the impact. Each time it hit the bottom of a trough, it would take in more water; water which would swirl around the cabin, spread over the deck, and sweep people, young and old, off their feet—many of them flat on their backs and in grave danger of being washed overboard. It was too rough and too deep for them to stand up. They were absolutely helpless. Grandma Atteberry was saved at the last minute from floating off the boat by Derwood Palmer.

Connie Palmer and Ronnie Atteberry, ages ten and eleven, thought it would be great fun to make their way toward the bow of the boat and let the waves wash over them. They were making their way along the side of the boat, holding on to the railing just beside the cabin, when a huge wave crashed into the bow and came rushing along the sides of the boat. It knocked Connie's feet out from under her and all but swept her under the pipe railing into the bay; only a last frantic grab at the railing saved her. And she didn't yet know how to swim. After finally regaining her place in the boat, she and Ronnie yelled at each other that they didn't think their going to the bow of the boat had been such a good idea after all.

Worst of all, Mr. Chester didn't dare turn the boat around, for with towering waves rushing upon the boat, if he tried to turn and was caught sideways, the next wave would wash the helpless passengers right off the boat.

Panic began to settle in as everyone began to realize how close they were to foundering. The children were crying, and the adults were praying for a miracle. Everyone begged Mr. Chester to turn his boat around. He was terrified himself, for now he realized how close they all were to sinking and the impossibility of turning the boat around before the next wave would swamp everyone.

At this juncture H. M. S. Richards, struggling to stay upright and braced against the back of the cabin, announced to all who could hear him, "We need to pray!" He outstretched his arms to heaven and prayed, asking the Lord that if it be His will, that He would please flatten out two waves so that the captain could turn the boat around—and, "Please, Lord, do it quick or we are all lost!"

Immediately afterwards, the passengers saw nothing but the next huge wave rushing upon them—but then, just in back of it, two waves flattened out into a smooth glassy calm. Immediately Mr. Chester turned on full power and turned the boat around. Just as he completed it, another wave smashed into the rear, but as soon as he was able to get his speed up, he was able to reach calmer waters, and they were then able to ride the waves back in to the port.

The rest of the afternoon turned into a prayer service of thanksgiving, for all realized that God had miraculously stepped in to save their lives. H. M. S. Richards summed up the harrowing experience best: "A boatload of people came ever so close to being down on the bottom of the bay." ❧

SECTION TWO

"Ask the animals, and they will teach you.
Ask the birds of the sky, and they will tell you.
Speak to the earth, and it will instruct you. . . .
They all know that the Lord has done this.
For the life of every living thing is in his hand,
and the breath of all humanity."
Job 12:7–10 (NLT)

*I*n emphasizing her testimony to the truth that God is still the living God who does things on earth, Mrs. Howard Taylor of the China Inland Mission told the story of an elderly convert named Li who did gospel work in the Yo-yang District and conducted a refuge for opium smokers who were seeking deliverance from that evil habit.

HIS DAILY BREAD

Mrs. Howard Taylor

*I*n Bible times, God used ravens and referred to them a number of times:

- "After another forty days, Noah opened the window he had made in the boat and released a raven that flew back and forth until the earth was dry" (Genesis 8:6, 7, NLT).
- "Then the LORD said to Elijah, 'Go to the east and hide by Kerith Brook at a place east of where it enters the Jordan River. Drink from the brook and eat what the ravens bring you, for I have commanded them to bring you food'" (1 Kings 17:2–4, NLT).
- "Who provides food for the ravens when their young cry out to God as they wander about in hunger?" (Job 38:41, NLT).

- "He feeds the wild animals, and the young ravens cry to him for food" (Psalm 147:9, NLT).
- "The eye that mocks a father and despises a mother will be plucked out by ravens of the valley and eaten by vultures" (Proverbs 30:17, NLT).
- "It [Edom] will be haunted by the horned owl, the hawk, the screech owl, and the raven" (Isaiah 34:11, NLT).
- "Look at the ravens. They don't need to plant or harvest or put food in barns because God feeds them" (Luke 12:24, NLT).

Have you ever wondered whether even God has favorites in the animal kingdom? And, in so many cases, why He gave ravens precedence over other species?

Soon after his conversion from idol worship, Li found the text "Covetousness, which is idolatry" [Colossians 3:5]. Determined not to fall into this kind of idolatry, he gave away all his property, and lived from day to day by the simple hospitality of those among whom he labored. In the opium relief work, he often saw hard times, but his trust was in the God who fed Elijah by the ravens. At one time, the old man had come to the end of his resources:

"Quite nearby, in the large temple of the village, lived a cousin who was priest in charge, and who, when he came to see his relative from time to time, would bring a little present of bread or millet from his ample store. The old man, on receiving these gifts, would always say, *'T'ien Fu tih en tien!'* ["My heavenly Father's grace"] meaning that it was through the care and kindness of God that these gifts were brought. But the priest did not approve of that way of looking at it, and at last remonstrated:

" 'Where does your heavenly Father's grace come in, I should like to know? The millet is mine. I bring it to you. And if I did not, you would very soon starve for all that He would care. He has nothing at all to do with it.'

" 'But it is my heavenly Father who puts it into your heart to care for me,' replied old Li.

" 'O, that is all very well!' interrupted the priest. 'We shall see what will happen if I bring the millet no more.' And so for a week or two he kept away, although his better nature prompted him to care for the old man, whom he could not but esteem for the works of mercy in which he was constantly engaged.

"As it happened, this was just the time in which dear old Li was especially short of supplies. At last there came a day when he had nothing left for another meal. The refuge was still empty, and he had not enough cash to buy even a morsel of bread. Kneeling alone in his room, he poured out his heart in prayer to God. He knew very well that the Father in heaven would not, could not, forget him; and after pleading for blessing on his work and upon the people all around him, he reminded the Lord of what the priest had said, asking that, for the honor of His own great name, He would send him that day his daily bread.

"Then and there the answer came. While the old man was still kneeling in prayer, he heard an unusual clamor and cawing and flapping of wings in the courtyard outside, and a noise as of something falling to the ground. He rose and went to the door to see what was happening. A number of ravens, which are common in that part of China, were flying all about in great commotion above him, and as he looked up, a large piece of meat fell at his very feet. One of the birds, chased by others, had dropped it just at that moment on that spot. [In the Orient one is accustomed to the sight of flocks of birds hovering over the marketplace, watching a chance to seize a piece of meat from a butcher's stall.]

"Thankfully the old man took up the unexpected portion, saying, 'My heavenly Father's kindness!' and then, glancing about him to see what had fallen before he came out, he discovered a large piece of Indian meal bread, all cooked and ready for eating. Another bird had dropped that also, and there was his dinner bountifully provided. Evidently, the ravens had been on a foraging expedition, and, overtaken by stronger birds, had let go their booty. But whose hand had guided them to relinquish their prize right above his little courtyard?

"With a wondering heart, overflowing with joy, the dear old man kindled a fire to prepare the welcome meal; and while the pot was still boiling, the door opened, and to his great delight his cousin, the priest, walked in.

" 'Look and see,' said the old man, smiling as he indicated the simmering vessel on the fire.

"For some time the priest would not lift the lid, feeling sure there was nothing boiling there but water; but at length the savory odor was unmistakable, and overcome by curiosity, he peeped into the earthen pot. What was his astonishment when the excellent dinner was revealed!

" 'Why,' he cried, 'where did you get this?'

" 'My heavenly Father sent it,' responded the old man, gladly. 'He put it into your heart, you know, to bring me a little millet from time to time; but when you would do so no longer, it was quite easy for Him to find another messenger.' And the whole incident, his prayer, and the coming of the ravens, was graphically told.

"The priest was so much impressed by what he saw and heard that he became from that time an earnest inquirer, and before long confessed his faith in Christ by baptism. He gave up his comfortable living in the temple for the blessed reality that now satisfied his soul. He supported himself as a teacher, became a much-respected deacon in the church, and during the Boxer troubles of 1900, endured terrible tortures and finally laid down his life for Jesus' sake." ❦

*D*obry, a Polish peasant, was about to be evicted with his family in the dead of winter. Desperate, Dobry prayed for God to save them, and then they sang "Give to the Winds Thy Fears."

Then there was a rap at the window.

Once again, God used one of His favorite messengers—a raven!

It was in the seventeenth century that Paul Gerhardt, a Lutheran pastor, wrote the blessed hymn "Give to the Winds Thy Fears." The familiar English translation renders two stanzas:

> Give to the winds thy fears,
>   Hope and be undismayed;
> God hears thy sighs and counts thy tears,
>   He shall lift up thy head.

> Through waves and clouds and storms,
>   He gently clears thy way;
> Wait thou His time, so shall this night
>   Soon end in joyous day.

It was amid trial and persecution that Gerhardt's trust had grown strong; and the hymns of faith and hope that poured from his soul have blessed and helped many another heart waiting through dark hours for God to "clear the way."

One lover of Gerhardt's hymn of trust was a Polish peasant named Dobry, who lived near Warsaw in the days of King Stanislaus (1764–1795). Dobry experienced a remarkable deliverance by a raven's visit, in which he recognized the direct intervention of the Lord. The story is told by S. W. Duffield, in his standard history of *English Hymns* (page 166):

"He had fallen into arrears with his rent, and his landlord was about to eject him from his home. It was the dead of winter, and the poor man had thrice appealed for mercy, but in vain. The next day was to see himself and his family homeless and hopeless in the midst of the snow. But Dobry kneeled down and prayed, and then they all sang this hymn. At length they came to the words, *'Dein werk kann niemand hindern'*:

> " 'Nothing Thy work suspending,
>   No foe can make Thee pause
> When Thou, Thine own defending,
>   Dost undertake their cause.'

"There was a rap at the window. Dobry went to it and opened it, and a raven which his grandfather had trained and set at liberty popped in with a valuable jeweled ring in its beak. The peasant took it at once to his minister, who identified it as the property of King Stanislaus, to whom he restored it.

"The king sent for Dobry, rewarded him handsomely, and the next year built him a new house, and gave him cattle from his own herds.

Over this house door, on an iron tablet, appears still, it is said, the effigy of a raven with a ring in its beak. Underneath are the first four lines of the stanza which was being sung: *'Weg hast du allerwegen,'* etc., which are thus rendered in the admirable version of Mrs. E. Charles:

" 'All means always possessing,
   Invincible in might;
Thy doings are all blessing,
   Thy goings are all light.' " ❧

*I*t seemed nothing on earth could save him.

    But a voice directed him to do a very strange thing . . .

    It continues to fascinate me that while we beg for long-term security in life, God's answer to our importuning tends to be just enough for today.

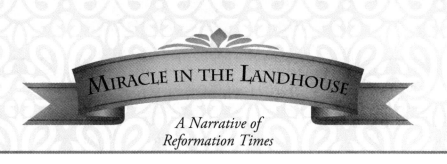

MIRACLE IN THE LANDHOUSE

*A Narrative of
Reformation Times*

*"O Jerusalem, Jerusalem, the city that kills the prophets and stones
God's messengers! How often I have wanted to gather your children
together as a hen protects her chicks beneath her wings, but you
wouldn't let me" (Matthew 23:37, NLT).*

Here is a narrative of Reformation times, taken from the life of Johannes Brenz, of Würtemberg (1499–1570):

"Of the many persecutions which Brenz had to suffer from the emperor on account of his steadfastness in the Protestant faith, the most perilous one to befall him occurred while he was a guest of Duke Ulric at Stuttgart.

"The emperor had learned of the whereabouts of Brenz, and commissioned a colonel to produce him, dead or alive. The duke, being apprised of this, warned Brenz, and let him go with the consolation, 'If God is pleased with you, he will deliver you.'

"Brenz, as if anticipating the peril, had already sent his four children to his friends. In the seclusion of his room he fell on his knees, and prayed to God for counsel and help. And he seemed to hear a voice saying: 'Take a loaf of bread, and go up through the Birkenwald

[the upper part of the city was so called at that time]; and where you find an open front door, go in and hide yourself under the roof.'

"Brenz did so. All the doors in that part of the city were closed until he came to the Landhouse [later the Reformed Church]. Here the door stood open. He entered without being seen by anyone. Under the roof was a large pile of wood, behind which he hid himself.

"The next day the imperial officer, with his Spanish soldiers, arrived in Stuttgart. Soldiers were at once stationed at all city gates, even at the exit of the duke's palace. They searched every house in the city, and finally the soldiers came to the Landhouse. Brenz perceived the clang of arms, and heard their loud talking and cursing as they went from room to room. They also came to his hiding-place under the roof, and thrust their spears through the woodpile behind which Brenz lay. But they did not find him, and two weeks later they left Stuttgart.

" 'Now they are gone, and, praise the Lord, they have not found him,' thus Brenz heard the people talk on the street below.

"But how was Brenz able to sustain his life during that long time? On the first day of his concealment, toward noon, about eleven o'clock, came a hen and laid an egg behind the woodpile. This she did every day till the end of his stay there. This egg served to quench his thirst, while the loaf of bread satisfied his hunger. The hen ceased coming on the day on which the soldiers departed." ❧

Have you given the horse its strength or clothed its neck with a flowing mane? Did you give it the ability to leap forward like a locust? Its majestic snorting is something to hear! It paws the earth and rejoices in its strength. When it charges to war, it is unafraid. It does not run from the sword. The arrows rattle against it, and the spear and javelin flash. Fiercely it paws the ground and rushes forward into battle when the trumpet blows. It snorts at the sound of the bugle. It senses the battle even at a distance. It quivers at the noise of the battle and the shout of the captain's commands" (Job 39:19–26, NLT).

Why the Horse Balked

Retold by H. W. Hastings

No, the horse did not, like Balaam's donkey, talk back to his master—but he certainly did something else!

Though the horse is known as one of the most intelligent of animals—clearly, this horse has a direct line to the throne of God!

A New England minister, years ago, wrote out for the late H. W. Hastings, of Boston, this story of deliverance:

His father was a man of faith, regularly committing the lives of all the household to God at the family altar. One day, in 1850, he started for the mill at Rockland, R.I., with a bag of rye to be ground into flour for the family bread. On the way the staid old family horse unaccountably balked on a bridge over a stream, and began to turn and back up. He kept on till the rear wheels of the wagon went over the log guard along the edge of the planks. The farmer jumped out, and the horse stood still, holding the front wheels catching on the log guard, so that the wagon did not go over, but the contents were thrown into the water. Neighbors helped to right the wagon up, and the grist was fished out. The minister says:

"There was a mystery about the transaction. The horse had showed no signs of fright, and had never acted so before. My father was perplexed. He had earnestly prayed only that morning that the angel of the Lord might encamp round about us that day, and here was this unaccountable accident.

"He returned home, and we went to work to dry our grain and prepare it for grinding; but when we spread out the rye upon a cloth in the sun to dry, we noticed, scattered through it all, fragments of a fine, glittering substance, which, on examination, proved to be glass. Thousands upon thousands of fine fragments mingled with those two bushels of rye— enough to cause the death of all the family if the grain had been ground and baked and eaten.

"We were amazed at this revelation; and with what grateful hearts we knelt around the family altar and thanked God for His wonderful providence which had so strangely preserved our lives."

He says they found on investigation that the rye had been kept for a time in an open barrel, and that above this workmen had been smoothing ax handles, using pieces of glass to scrape and polish the wood. In this way particles of glass had been ground off, and fallen down through and into the rye. This was unnoticed when the grain was emptied into the sack to be taken to the mill when bread was needed.

*I*f even ravens and hens can be used by God, how about much, much, much smaller creatures—such as a mere insect?

Spiders—just a pesky insect to be brushed away or smashed. Or are they? Somehow, after reading this story, I marvel that even something so tiny is capable of orchestrating commands from God.

SAVED BY A SPIDER'S WEB

Baxendale

"The spider taketh hold with her hands, and is in kings' palaces"
(Proverbs 30:28).

An old work, Baxendale's *Dictionary of Anecdotes,* preserves the following record of the times of 1662. The experience is almost the same as one recorded of a French Huguenot, in the days of the St. Bartholomew's Day massacre.

"A story is related—in connection with the ejectment of the two thousand ministers from the Church of England—of Henry Havers, of Catherine Hall, Cambridge. Being pursued by enemies who sought to apprehend him, he sought refuge in a malt house, and crept into the kiln. Immediately afterward, he observed a spider fixing the first line of a large and beautiful web across the narrow entrance. The web being placed directly between him and the light, he was so much struck with the skill of the insect weaver, that for a while he forgot his own imminent danger; but by the time the network had crossed and re-crossed the mouth of the kiln in every direction, the pursuers came to search for him. He listened as they approached, and distinctly overheard one of them say: 'It is of no use to look in there; the old villain could never be there. Look at that spider's web. He could never have got in there without breaking it.' " ✺

SECTION THREE

"When they arrived at the Jordan, they began cutting down trees. But as one of them was chopping, his ax head fell into the river. 'Ah, my lord!' he cried. 'It was a borrowed ax!' 'Where did it fall?' the man of God asked. When he showed him the place, Elisha cut a stick and threw it into the water. Then the ax head rose to the surface and floated. 'Grab it,' Elisha said to him. And the man reached out and grabbed it."
2 Kings 6:4–7 (NLT)

*L*ittle did anyone realize that rainy morning that before the day was over, each of them would be staring death in the face.

After I heard my nephew tell this story to our family, I harassed him so much that finally he wrote down for us this story of a life-changing day.

SNATCHED FROM THE GREEN RIVER

Byron Palmer

It was 6:00 A.M. when the phone rang. It was Gary, our pastor and river guide, and he came right to the point: "I'm sorry, Byron, but your son, Alex, will have to stay home today."

"Why?"

"Because, after days of persistent, drenching rain, the river flow will just be too high for him. He's too inexperienced."

Even though I knew, deep down, that Gary was right, I just dreaded telling our eleven-year-old that the river trip he'd been anticipating for so long wouldn't happen for him.

This would not be my first white-water rafting expedition, as Gary had organized previous trips on various western Washington rivers, such as the Tieton, Wenatchee, and Skykomish. I surveyed my gear: black wet suit, booties and gloves, a blue life vest, and bright yellow helmet. Alex took it better than I thought he would, so I grabbed a bite of breakfast, packed a lunch, hugged and kissed my family goodbye, and headed out, eager to start the adventure. It was to be more adventure than any of us had bargained for.

On that soggy April morning, our group gathered in the parking lot of our church, then headed out to Flaming Geyser State Park. Here we consolidated our gear into a couple of SUVs and piled in. Then we drove thirteen winding miles to Kanaskat-Palmer State Park. Here we inflated our rafts, were thoroughly briefed by our guide, and prayed that God would guide and protect us. Then we carried our two rafts down to the riverbank, got in, and were soon on our way.

This stretch of the Green River flows through the Green River Gorge—through what locals have hailed as the "hanging gardens" or "Jurassic Park." It flows through a narrow moss and tree-lined canyon with the look and feel of a rain forest. The Green River is notorious for its challenging rapids, which are typically classified as Class III and IV. Rapids are categorized by their difficulty and danger on a scale of I–VI, in Roman numerals. Placid waters, with only a few ripples, a few small waves, and few if any obstructions are Class I. Class VI rapids are extreme, violent, and considered not commercially raftable and often include waterfalls. Confined by its high, narrow canyon, the currents of the Green River are propelled by the speed of its water ripping between its walls and over the boulders. The Class IV rapids of the Green River have such monikers as Mercury, Pipeline, Nozzle, and Seeing God and have complicated passageways that must be skillfully navigated with intent to follow the correct path through the torrential flow. Interspersed among the Class IV rapids are twenty-five other rapids rated as Class III. These still demand precise maneuvering and often drench the occupants of the raft.

There were nine paddlers in the two crews of our group: Gary (our guide), Mert, Alan, Jeac, and I were in the first raft; Heney, who was Jeac's brother, Roxanne, and two others made up the crew of the second raft.

The guide of each raft powered the oars that both steered and helped propel the raft. The remaining occupants used paddles in response to commands barked by the guide to maneuver through the currents. The steady rain and churning waves kept both crews actively paddling while anticipating the river's next move. The upper part of the river is not as steep or narrow, so the current is gentler, and it provides a good warm-up for the Class IV rapids to follow.

Ninety some minutes into our trip we stopped for lunch. In one of the bends in the river, there was a small beach with quiet water. We reflected on our float so far and shared stories between the crews of the two rafts. None of us noticed the subtle rising of the river during lunch, and only in retrospect did it occur to us that before lunch we had been ahead of a surge of intensifying current. We would later learn that the Howard A. Hanson Reservoir upstream had reached its capacity, and the water management engineers had begun releasing water in their part of controlling the resources of the Green River Watershed. Gary noticed the effect as soon as we got back on the river but didn't say anything because there was no way out of the gorge but downstream. To the rest of us, it simply felt as though we were beginning the Class IV section of the river. As the power of the current began to build and rapids came more frequently, our guide began issuing orders. The paddling now required greater effort on our part to navigate.

"Forward paddle!"

"Back paddle—left!"

"Forward paddle—hard!"

Gary shouted commands in quick succession as we jockeyed left, then right, then built up speed to crash through a gigantic wave.

Suddenly our raft dipped into a hole the size of an inverted Volkswagen. The exit curl of that wave eclipsed the river downstream, and its angle flipped our raft with ferocity. *Wham!* The raft instantly ejected us into the glacial runoff. Now out of the raft, we became swimmers. The overdose of adrenaline blocked out the rush of cold in spite of our thick wet suits. We grabbed for the raft's perimeter rope, the now inverted raft remaining our best flotation device. We would be safer on the upstream side of the raft with us following the raft downriver; the raft would provide a significant bumper between us and the boulders defining the flow of the current. Most of us had worked our way to the backside of the raft. Mert, however, was missing.

I clung tightly to the raft's perimeter rope. There were three remaining Class IV rapids yet to come. Ice-cold water filled my lungs as I gasped for air. The desperate circumstances shut out my sense of time and distance. Between waves, I coughed and spit out the water threatening to drown me. My timing was always off. I would no sooner clear my airways, ready for the next lung-full of fresh air, when that breath would be replaced by the next wave, force-feeding my windpipe. After what seemed like thirty minutes of nature-imposed waterboarding, another monster wave ripped the raft's rope from the grasp of my gloved hands. When I surfaced again, I saw with dread that the raft was now twenty feet downstream. The river, it seemed, was determined to swallow me. I was alone in a Class IV river with nothing but my life vest to keep me afloat. Gary's pointing arm and his shrieking voice directed me toward the riverbank. I needed to get out of the river and onto the shore to avoid smashing into rocks or being pinned or sucked under by their swirling currents and to stay clear of the fallen trees, "strainers" or "sieves" that could snag part of a wet suit or life vest and hold a swimmer under water.

The occupants of our raft would later learn that a hundred yards behind us, the second raft had already capsized. The occupants were rudely hurled into the water. Some were clinging tenaciously to the rope skirting the raft; others, who had separated from it, were furiously trying to swim their way back to rejoin the others. The members of the second group were also trying to get our attention in hopes of being pulled aboard our raft—that is, until they witnessed our own capsizing. We were all now ripping through rapids as if shot from a fire hose. The roar of the river and the demands

of our concentration on our own situation, however, prevented us from knowing the plight of the others.

The Green River has claimed its share of lives—roughly 3 a year, with 112 more in area waters plus another 450 to 500 near drownings. At high flow, the Green River is ferocious and, like other fast rivers, generates what are known in the rafting world as "hydraulics"— massive water swirls that include rapids, whirlpools, undercurrents, and other such diabolical flows. The force of those hydraulics can pin someone to a rock, drive an individual to the bottom of the river, or simply, and too often terminally, recirculate the unfortunate swimmer back through the same churning froth over and over until it is too late for rescue. Low flow can also be treacherous because it can expose swimmers to more sieves. At any level, fallen logs, along or across a river, create "strainers" like a giant comb letting nothing but water through the branches penetrating the torrent at every angle and trapping the hapless. Whether high flow, low flow, or somewhere in between, many of the region's drowning deaths are due to the cold. In April, May, and June, rivers are still being fed by snowpack and glaciers.

Floating on my back face up, the "hanging gardens" on the near-vertical walls of the gorge looked like they would become my prison walls. My life vest felt barely adequate. My body angled toward the shore, and I began backstroking, slowed by the stiffness of my thick wet suit. I had been swimming in the middle of the river (which spanned a hundred feet in width). Desperate and feeling hopeless, I felt as if I would need to swim five hundred miles to reach a bank. My greatest fear was that I would crash into the boulders or become tangled in a strainer and drown.

On my first backstroke, I sent up a prayer: "God, please send angels. I need help!" I wondered how much more water I could take in without drowning. On my second backstroke, the river grew quiet. The spray of the waves subsided. For the first time since being plunged into the river, I inhaled deeply without sucking in water. Suddenly, aware of a change, I opened my eyes. No longer was I in the middle of a churning, frothing river. Somehow, beyond my comprehension and ability, I had mysteriously settled in a harmless eddy behind a rock on the bank of this surging, ripping river. My eyes scanned upward. The nearly vertical bluff would be the only path out. The rock before me towered so high I couldn't even see whether there were further walls behind. *Why didn't I major in rock climbing in college?* I thought wryly. Exhausted but determined to press on, I offered a quick prayer of thanks to God for the water rescue and extended my arm to begin scaling the boulder.

My fingers found a small crack. Reaching up the minicrevasse to the full extension of my arms would take me one-quarter, perhaps one-third, of the way to the crown of the rock, and I lunged to break free of the water. I lost my grip and plunged back into the water and now felt the icy cold on my face as I sank deep beneath the surface. I refused to let this setback discourage me. I tried again. Another fall, and I wondered how many

times I could spare the energy to do this. While the wet suit protected me from the cold water and from the abrasion of the rocks, it made me feel very stiff and heavy. I wondered whether Mert had survived and thought about the rest of the group as well. I also pondered how I was going to get out of the gorge. I tightened my fingers into the crack once more and jammed my toes as deep as they would go. I sent up another prayer, and this time my grip held. Five feet to go and I could look down on the river. When I reached the top, I was completely exhausted. I collapsed on the top of this mossy rock in the rain for what seemed like fifteen minutes. Ingesting all that water made me feel nauseous. I still didn't know the fate of my companions, so I prayed for them. I prayed especially hard for Mert. I couldn't allow the "what ifs" to enter my mind. I needed to focus again.

What time was it?

How long had I been in the water?

Was I bleeding or injured anywhere?

I took an inventory. All my body parts were accounted for. My paddle rested on the far side of the rock. I concluded that I could actually reach it without jeopardy of falling back in the river. It would serve as a lightweight walking stick. I surveyed the bluff above me and the river below me.

My eye caught a red object floating on the river. It looked like a red basketball in the current. It was actually a helmet being worn by a kayaker, his kayak and body obscured while torpedoing the waves of the rapids. I thought for a moment that I could call to him for help, but in an instant he was gone.

An eight-inch-diameter downed log lay between the boulder I was standing on and the bluff I needed to climb. It looked precarious. I scanned the bank—too far to jump. I considered the water below. This slippery log had to suffice. Inching out on the log, I was leery of its strength. Crossing the log proved to be uneventful as long as I could keep my mind off the disaster it would be if the log broke with me halfway across it. I was on the bank now, and the bluff looked much steeper than it had from the rock. Working methodically from fern to tree to root to fern, my feet would climb three steps, but the sliding, shifting soil would limit my progress to mere inches, maybe a foot of upward progress at a time, nothing more. A topographical map of the area later showed 280 feet from the river to the rim of the gorge. It seemed like forever! Rests were frequent. Any hint of cold now escaped me, replaced by perspiration. I needed a restroom but could neither afford the body heat nor squander the remaining daylight to stop and shimmy out of the wet suit even for a little bit. I climbed on.

When I finally reached the top, I was faced with another decision: Which direction would I go? The only evidence of civilization was the distant sound of a chain saw. Maybe I would follow that sound. When lost in the outback, one should head downhill. That would take me back to the river—bad plan! My mind raced ahead of me, knowing that my remaining daylight was limited, and I had no idea how much I had left or what time it was getting to be. Was daylight fading or were denser clouds simply delivering heavier rain or darkening the sky?

Or was I that deep in the woods? I had to press on. Eventually, it would get dark, and since I was wet, I knew that sooner or later I would get cold. I had an overwhelming desire to enjoy the heat while it lasted, thinking how nice it would be if I could store it up for later.

The forest at the top was thicker with heavier undergrowth than I imagined. I had to make a straight line to somewhere. Away from the river seemed reasonable to me. How long would it take for a search party to give up trying to find me on the river? Would they even try to search the adjoining forest? I looked at the moss on the trees to try to orient myself, thinking that perhaps I would be able to make a straighter line if I kept the moss pointing the same way throughout my trek. Since here moss grows on all sides of the trees rather than the more typical north side, this strategy would not help me now. As I stepped over downed trees and trudged steadily onward through the forest, the roar of the river slowly receded to a whisper in the background. I was making headway! The forest thinned, and the world grew brighter. A dirt road lay ahead, and I would be able to pick up the pace. I walked as briskly as possible in my stiff wet suit. I wondered what people would think when they saw me. I looked more like a visiting alien than a survivor of a rafting trip gone awry with my black seven-mil wet suit, blue life vest, and yellow helmet. I didn't care, as long as somebody found me.

The forest gave way to cultivated timber. *I must be on a logging road,* I thought. It either led to a public road or deeper into the wilderness, but it went *somewhere,* so I plodded stiffly on. I continued praying for my friends. I now felt I would be safe, grateful for signs of man's intrusion on the wild. My neoprene booties were still holding up, I thought approvingly. I trudged ahead, not even slowing to check their soles, only trying to walk on the smoothest part of the trail. I wondered whether anybody would cross my way or whether they would take notice if they saw me.

Finally, up ahead, a gate led to a paved road. My thoughts went immediately to my friends. Did they all get off the river? Did they survive? Now that I was on a public road, would there be any traffic? Which way should I walk? I chose to turn right. I held my blue-and-yellow paddle up and waved it at the first vehicle I saw. The driver of the pickup slowed, stopped, and invited me into his truck. As he drove, I shared my story with him, grateful for someone to talk to. The man dropped me off at the local convenience store and went in with me to make sure I could hang out there until help arrived. The store clerk graciously allowed me to make a few calls. One call went to 9-1-1. One call went to my wife, and one call went to Rhonda, our guide's wife.

Finally, after reuniting with the rest of the group, the full story was pieced together. Right after capsizing, Mert had come up on the downstream side of the raft and hadn't worked his way around to the upstream side until after my separation from the group. Most of those on my raft had experienced at least one of the Class IV rapids while swimming. Two of them—Gary and Mert—had been spewed through the Nozzle. Everyone else had crawled or washed ashore above the Nozzle, including the crew from the other raft. The rafts were both gone, washed downstream.

Perhaps the most desperate situation was that of Heney, who had elected to throw his raincoat on over his life jacket but with the hood of the raincoat under his helmet. The current used this raincoat like a sail to drive him to the bottom of the river, where he found himself running full speed along the bottom of the river while trying desperately to shed the raincoat. Heney finally got the coat unzipped and off his arms, but it still clung to his head by his helmet. We were all grateful it didn't snag on a rock or branch. There was no way he could have beat the river in that case.

Some of the rafters stumbled into some off-roaders out in their 4x4s who took mercy on them and took them to a house along a more civilized stretch of the river. It didn't take long before the commotion next door reunited eight of our nine from the two rafts. I was still the missing man. No one yet knew of my fate, and they all feared the worst. I was the only one separated from the group and totally on my own.

The Washington Highway Patrol and a local sheriff's deputy both answered the call to retrieve me from the convenience store. The deputy drove me to the house where my companions were waiting. I only visited a little with the deputy because he seemed more interested in the chatter of his police radio. There appeared to be reports of river rafters climbing into neighborhood backyards. The radio directed him to a home where we had to work our way around three or four ambulances, a couple of fire trucks, a lot of law enforcement, and a handful of media. I made my way to the front door, where I was able to dodge the reporters and get inside.

My friends greeted me with hugs and enthusiastic cheering. Everybody was very solemn but thrilled that we were together at last and no one was hurt beyond minor scrapes and bruises.

An ambulance then drove us to the put-in where our SUVs had been parked. In a short time, we were all together again, offering prayers of thanks and praise to God for His protection. Those prayer sessions were repeated several times both at home and at church over the next few weeks.

Sometime later we learned that the release of water from the reservoir had nearly doubled the flow of water in the river, taking the flow rate well above what is considered runnable. That flow had caught up with us during lunch. While we waited for our rides, a park ranger met us at the Kanaskat-Palmer State Park and took it upon himself to chastise us for our recklessness and to share the history of the river's toll on human life. He made it clear that we never should have run the river that day. We tried to tell him that we had monitored the river flow for several days. Yet in retrospect, it wasn't enough. We were fortunate to be alive. And, strangely, his searing, sobering words made sense in stark contrast to the alternative.

Later that summer I was back on the river. I have continued to raft but now ask more questions and check conditions more thoroughly for myself. The beauty of the area rivers, the

challenge, and the exhilaration continue to draw me to the sport.

A strange aftereffect from the experience was my adverse reaction to drinking fountains. The smell of water from the drinking fountain triggered an unpleasant reflex in me, and that sensation lingered in my mind for a couple of years with every drink I took, the effect tapering over time to a rare déjà vu as late as ten years after the fact. God spared us all, and some of us in miraculous ways. Recently, my son turned twenty-three. I shudder to think of the possible outcome had he gone on that trip. I am both amazed and moved by the concern that drove our God-fearing friends to their knees and compelled them to urge our guide in the most persuasive terms to have our son remain behind.

God has a plan for our lives, and it is my desire to live that plan for Him. ❧

*T*he captain, first to board the ill-fated ship, took one look at the survivors, lifted his hat, and said solemnly, "Now I believe that there is a God in heaven!"

I included this old story because it reminds me that no matter how desperate the situation, no matter how impossible the odds may seem, if it be His will, God can be depended upon to answer such pleas for help.

A Rescue at Sea

Helen A. Steinhauer

In the *Youth's Instructor* of November 8, 1894, Miss Helen A. Steinhauer told of a voyage by sailboat from the island of Jamaica to New Orleans.

Her parents were Moravian missionaries, and their health failing, it was decided that they should go to a cooler place, and they shipped by sailing vessel bound for a Mississippi port. Their ship was driven by a storm far from its course, and then a dead calm settled down, making progress impossible. It was many years ago, when there were fewer ships abroad on the Mexican Gulf waters than in our time. The ship was provisioned for but a few days, and soon it was necessary to ration the passengers and crew. Miss Steinhauer says:

"As the days lengthened into weeks, our sufferings were extreme. I remember gnawing at a kid glove for what nutriment it might contain. We were put upon rations of half a ship biscuit and half a pint of water in every twenty-four hours,—a very small allowance of food, and a still smaller one of drink beneath a semi-tropical sun. . . .

"Some gulped their portion of water as soon as it was given them; others hugged it to them with fierce eagerness, as long as they could, dreading lest a stronger hand might snatch it away. At length our tongues became so swollen from protracted thirst that we could scarcely close our mouths. My mother found that dipping cloths into the sea and binding them dripping wet about our throats, afforded some relief; but oh, how maddening it was to see water, water, everywhere, yet not a drop to drink! Our sufferings from hunger were extreme, but the suffering from thirst was great beyond expression!

"When four weeks had nearly dragged their slow length along, it was decided that to make our scant allowance last one day longer, some of our number were to be thrown overboard. The lot was to be cast at night, but the result was not to be made known till just before the food was given out, in the hope that deliverance might come before the measure was put into execution. . . .

"My father and a Spanish gentleman slept on deck, but my mother and I, being the only females on board, besides the captain's wife and three women in the hold, retired to our berths in the cabin.

"Of course many and importunate prayers had been offered all along, but my mother determined to spend the entire night in supplication, which she accordingly did. At early daylight she sank into the sleep of exhaustion, from which she was awakened by my father's voice, saying:

" 'My dear, we think that we see a sail.'

" 'Oh,' exclaimed my mother, wearily, 'it will pass us by, like all the rest!' We had been constantly tantalized by the sight of vessels passing like dim specks on the western horizon, but so far away that we could not hail them, nor could they see our signals of distress. Then recollecting her night's occupation, she repentantly added: 'No, God forgive me! It is an answer to my prayer; it will come to our relief.'

" 'Don't be too sure, wife,' said my father, gently; 'I would not have you disappointed. If it be God's will for us, it will come to our relief.'

" 'It is His will,' replied my mother, confidently. 'I am sure that help is at hand.'

"As quickly as possible we dressed and crawled up the narrow hatchway. I shall never forget the sight that presented itself as we got on deck. There, on the side of the vessel nearest the object from which the hoped-for relief was to come, were gathered the entire ship's company. Not a word was spoken, but as the naked eye could not yet discern anything, in breathless silence the ship's spyglass was passed from one to the other, that each might see.

"It certainly seemed as if it were a vessel. Yes; now we were quite sure of the fact. But would it come this way? Or must we again see it vanish out of sight, like the ship of a dream?

"No; it came nearer and nearer, and nearer still. Soon we could see it with the naked eye. Signals we could not make; we were far too weak and helpless. But it came on, nevertheless, straight and true, directly bearing down upon us. By and by they hailed us:

" 'Ship ahoy!'

"But not a man aboard had strength of voice sufficient to make reply.

"Still they came on nearer, nor did they stop till within easy distance of our luckless vessel, when a boat was let down, into which stepped four men, one evidently the captain. The supreme tension of that moment is indelibly impressed upon my mind, child though I was at the time.

"He was the first to board us, and as he set foot on our deck and saw our wretched plight, he lifted his hat and said, solemnly:

" 'Now I believe that there is a God in heaven!'

"It proved to be one of the small steamers that tow sailing vessels into the harbor, across the bar. By the rules that then bound them (they may be changed now, I cannot say), they were not allowed to go beyond a certain distance out of port to look for vessels needing their assistance. But this was the strange story the captain told:

"After he had gone the full limit, he felt unaccountably impelled to go still farther, although there was not a vessel in sight. His mate remonstrated with him, reminding him of the fine to which he laid himself liable if he persisted.

" 'Can't help it! I've *got* to go on!' was his only reply.

"By and by he became desperately seasick, a thing which had not happened to him before in twenty years, and he was compelled to take his berth, 'like a landlubber!' and yet he refused to turn back, but bade them push still farther out to sea. Then his crew mutinied; for they were growing short of provisions, and determined to take the matter in their own hands, thinking that he must have lost his senses.

"At this his distress of mind became agonizing, and he implored them to go on, promising them that if they saw nothing to justify his action by sunrise the next morning, he would give up, and promptly alter his course.

"The men reluctantly consented; and when day dawned, the man at the masthead reported a black, motionless object far out to sea.

" 'Make for it!' exclaimed the captain, emphatically. 'That's what we've come after.'

"And at that instant his seasickness left him, and he took the post of command as before. On reaching us and seeing our emaciated forms and general wretchedness, although he had been an infidel for many years, the conviction forced itself upon him with overwhelming power that he had been supernaturally guided, and that there *was* a God in heaven; and later on, when he learned how my feeble mother had spent the night, he broadened his view to include the fact that He was a prayer-hearing and prayer-answering God."

It was exactly four weeks from the day they left Kingston, Jamaica, until they arrived at New Orleans. ❧

*M*iss Endicott was deathly seasick. Unable to keep down anything but oranges—and now here was the very last one. And the ship was yet in mid-ocean! Was her case hopeless?

Through the years I have stumbled on a number of memorable stories having to do with oranges, for before refrigeration they were so rare in nontropical countries that they were prized above any other food. But this is the first story of its kind I have ever unearthed: Doesn't it boggle your mind to conceive of a God of all the numberless swirling universes going to this much trouble to rescue a woman from seasickness?

ORANGES FROM HEAVEN

Miriam Kershaw

People often exclaim, "Wonders will never cease!" And it is quite true. How can wonders cease with such a wonderful God in heaven, with whom nothing is too hard—nothing impossible?

Miss Endicott was on board a ship bound for America. Tossed up and down and all ways at once by the big waves of the Atlantic, she lay in her berth nearly dead from seasickness. She shuddered at the thought of food, yet she must eat something in order to stay alive. After trying various things, it was discovered that she could take oranges. So all the oranges in the ship were claimed by the kindhearted stewardess for the benefit of this poor lady, and day after day she was kept supplied with some small slices, for she could eat very little.

At last, one stormy day, when the vessel was pitching and tossing more violently than ever, the stewardess came into the cabin with a troubled face.

"I don't know what we are going to do for you now," she said, "for this is the very last orange we have left"; and she showed her the treasure—more valuable at that moment than its own weight in gold.

Miss Endicott's face, however, did not reflect the cloud on that of her kind friend. She took the fruit thankfully. "What I have to do now," she said, "is to make the most of this. If I have to die, I am not afraid; but all the same, I know God can send me some more, if it is His will."

Send more oranges in mid-ocean! thought the stewardess, though she would not distress the invalid by uttering her thoughts aloud. They were something like those of the great man of old, when Elisha promised that the next day there should be abundance of food in Samaria in a time of terrible famine. "Behold, if the Lord would make windows in heaven, might this thing be?" [2 Kings 7:2].

It is stormy enough, thought the good woman, as she went on deck; *if it would rain oranges, the poor dear might be supplied—but hardly otherwise! No, no, I don't see how she can possibly get more.*

She eagerly cast quick glances over the tossing billows, and sighed as she thought of the sufferer.

Miss Endicott calmly ate the orange that had been peeled and sliced ready for her, and then closed her eyes again. Hour after hour she lay there, sleepless and suffering, but resting her heart—in spite of seeming impossibilities—on the sweet word, "Your Father knoweth that ye have need of these things" [Luke 12:30].

Suddenly, she was aroused from the dull stupor of misery by strange sounds overhead. Scurrying feet, excited voices, queer sounds of hauling up the ship's side—what could be happening?

"Here they are!" cried the stewardess, running into the cabin carrying a dish of large juicy oranges in either hand. "Here they are, you see! Isn't it wonderful? I am sure it is a miracle!"

"Oh!" And Miss Endicott's wan face lighted up with thankfulness. "Where did they come from?"

"Come from?" said the laughing stewardess. "I will tell you. They were just rained down from heaven on purpose for you."

And then she explained.

"A vessel had been seen flying signals of distress. Their captain steamed up as near as he could, hailed the skipper, and was told they were nearly starving; all their provisions were gone.

"The good skipper thereupon overhauled the stores on board, a boat was lowered, and as much food as could be spared was sent to the crew in distress.

"And what do you think," said the stewardess. "They were so grateful that they sent us baskets and baskets full of their cargo—because they had nothing else to give—and their cargo was oranges! Now you will have enough and to spare for the rest of the voyage."

"Can God furnish a table in the wilderness?" [Psalm 78:19], the murmuring, forgetful Israelites asked of old.

"Can God provide oranges in midocean?" the faithful stewardess had asked.

"I know God can," the faithful invalid had declared, "and I know He will, if He thinks it is best"; and again it had come true.

"According to your faith be it unto you" [Matthew 9:29]. The stewardess had learned a lesson. She never forgot that day when God thus arranged that a ship full of oranges should be brought into the middle of the Atlantic Ocean just to feed one single child of His who trusted Him. ❧

G randma always told the best stories! However, on this particular evening, Grandma decided to, one more time, tell the children about a day that was almost her last.

Today, we are so spoiled by technology that it's hard for us to conceive of living in a world where a balloon ride was perceived as being exciting. In this story, who caused Brother to grab the one piece of rope that could save the two children?

Well, children, what shall our story be about tonight?" asked Ruth and Ted's grandma.

"Oh, tell us about the time when Father got his first new suit of clothes," pleaded Ted.

"That would be very interesting, but I'd rather hear about the time you and Great-uncle Robert went for a balloon ride," said Ruth.

"Would you really like to hear that tonight? I have told it so many times I'm sure you know every detail by heart, but if you really want to hear it again, I'll do my best."

"Please do," cried both children eagerly. "We aren't tired of hearing that story."

"Well, it was a long time ago, when I was a little girl, and your great-uncle was just a little older than I. It was one bright Fourth of July morning when Father and Mother decided to give us children an extra treat by taking us to the village for the day. We were very happy, for we always enjoyed being with our schoolmates and friends. Also there were firecrackers, races, and slippery poles to climb."

"Uncle tore his best suit one time climbing a slippery pole, didn't he?" interrupted Ted.

"Yes, he did, son, but we must not get away from our story," smiled Grandma. "We children had a lovely time all morning, playing with the other boys and girls. This was a rare occasion for your uncle and me, because we lived quite a distance from any other children in the country. At noon we ate a hearty dinner, for we were very hungry. After dinner we wandered over to watch the people going up in the balloon. You have never seen a really truly balloon, but when we were children, these were quite common, especially on such occasions as a fair."

"What did they look like, Grandma?" inquired Ruth. "Were they like the big round rubber ones we get sometimes?"

"No, not exactly like that, but you may have seen them flying as anchored advertisements in the city. They are sometimes used in that way."

"Oh, yes, we have!" Ted and Ruth exclaimed together.

"Well, this one looked about the same, only there was a basket fastened on the lower end of the big round bag where passengers rode. We watched the people go up for some time. The caretakers had a strong rope attached to the balloon, with which they pulled it down after it had gone up as far as they wished it to go."

"My, it must have been lots of fun to go for

a ride like that, Grandma," observed Ted.

"Well, that is just what your great-uncle and I thought, but of course we had no idea Father would let us. To our surprise, he asked us if we would like to go up. Mother was rather afraid to let us, but after watching others having such a fine time, she yielded. How overjoyed we were to think we were going for a really truly balloon ride!

"Father paid the man, and helped us into the basket. He told us not to be afraid and to have a good ride. Then the man let the balloon go. Up it went; my, what fun it was! The people grew smaller and smaller. *Snap!* What was that noise? The man had started to pull the balloon down, but the rope had broken. Instead of going down, we went up! up! up! At first it was lots of fun. We were really sailing through the air like birds. After a while it grew tiresome, and we wished we were back with our father and mother. As the hours passed, we became tired and more lonesome. It was not a bit of fun now. We became hungrier and hungrier. My, it seemed as if we had *never* eaten anything, even if it was only a few hours since dinnertime."

"Wasn't it terribly cold up there?" questioned Ruth. "I have heard that people get quite cold when they go up in airplanes if they don't dress especially warm for it."

"Yes, it *was* cold. You see, we had on only light summer clothes. I began to cry because I was so cold and frightened. 'Will we ever see dear Papa and Mama again?' I wailed to Uncle Robert.

"Uncle Robert tried to comfort me, but at last he lost courage too. Then to add to our misery, it began to mist. No, not rain, but just a fine mist that makes a person cold and damp. Uncle was a regular little man, for he took off his thin jacket and put it over me, but of course it was soon wet clear through.

"We wondered what Mother and Father were doing. 'They must have gone home long ago. My, they must be very worried! . . . The cows have been milked by now. I don't believe I'll ever whine when I have to go for the cows—*if* I get home,' Robert moaned.

" 'Neither will I ever complain about washing dishes and sweeping again,' I cried. 'But—but do you think we'll ever see our dear parents again?'

" 'Say, sis, let's pray,' suggested Uncle Robert finally. 'You know Mother has always told us to pray when we are in trouble. She says if we only have faith in God, He will answer our prayers. I'll pray first, Ruth; then you pray.'

"So we bowed our heads way up there in the air, and we prayed simple, childish petitions for God to take care of us and bring us safely home. After we finished, we felt better. We curled down in the bottom of the basket, close together to keep warm. It was getting dark, and after a few minutes we were fast asleep."

"But what were your father and mother doing all this time?" interrupted Ruth. "They must have been terribly frightened. I'm sure *my* mother would have been."

"Well, Mother and Father *were* worried.

They stayed in town as long as they could, but toward evening they had to go home to do chores. The story of the lost balloon soon spread throughout the countryside. That night the neighbors gathered at our house for an earnest season of prayer. This comforted Mother's heart somewhat, but still she couldn't forget her two lone children adrift in the balloon. There was little sleeping at home that night. Telegrams were sent all over the country, asking people to look out for a balloon with two children in it.

"We children slept soundly all night, but as the dawn of day broke, we awoke. At first we rubbed our eyes and wondered where we were. Brother grabbed a little piece of rope that hung down from the gas sack to pull himself up. At first we didn't notice any difference, but in a short time we realized that we were going down. How thankful we were to know we were actually descending inch by inch nearer to dear mother earth. We were so grateful we couldn't help thanking God for His guiding hand over us throughout the long, dark night and for the descending of the balloon. Then brother pulled the cord a little more, and the balloon started to descend faster."

"But Grandma, what made the balloon go down?" inquired Ted.

"Well, we didn't know then, only that it had something to do with the pulling of the string, but since then I have found out that when we pulled the string, it opened a little valve in the balloon that let out some of the gas. When the gas was let out, it made the balloon heavier than the air; so it had to come down.

"Soon all the neighborhood was ablaze with the story of the descending balloon, and all were out eagerly looking for it. Our parents received word of it, and hastened to the place where the balloon was coming down. But another fear gripped their hearts now—there was a lake near where we were coming down! 'Will they land in the water?' was the question on everyone's lips."

"How did it happen that you didn't come down in the lake?" eagerly gasped Ruth.

"Well, this was another direct answer to prayer. Our folks were praying earnestly for our safe deliverance, and to their joy, a strong wind came up and drove us away from the lake, so that we landed safely in a nearby field. Our parents were there to help us out of our ship, in which we had had such a long ride. What a reunion that was, and how thankful we were to God for answering our prayers! But, children, you must go to bed now. It is after eight o'clock. I didn't realize my story was taking so much time."

"All right, Grandma, we'll go without fussing if you'll promise to tell us another story tomorrow night."

And soon both Ruth and Ted were fast asleep. Who can wonder what they dreamed of: balloons and lakes and—yes, of answered prayers too! ❧

*W*hat was wrong with the engine? Without prayer, it wouldn't start; with prayer, it would!

A plane engine, being an inanimate object, would seem to be outside of God's control. But in this faith-affirming story by my brother-in-law, we discover that even here, God is both capable and willing to somehow reach through molecules to exert His will.

In 1975, my missionary family and I moved to Zaire, which is now the Democratic Republic of Congo. It is a huge country, with diverse climate and land forms: high mountains, deep lakes, glaciers, and equatorial jungle and volcanoes. My job was to fly a Cessna 185 to and fro carrying freight or passengers as needed.

My plane mainly served the northern mountainous area of Zaire, but I had flights going from Kinshasa, the capital, in the far west to Kisangani in the north; to Lubumbashi and the Zaire Union headquarters in the south; to Nairobi, Kenya, in East Africa. It is indeed a beautiful land.

One particular flight had to do with a request to deliver a family from the Songa Mission hospital (south-central Zaire) to Nairobi, Kenya, to connect with a flight to the United States. I flew down to Songa and loaded up their luggage. Then we flew back northeast to the mountainous area of Goma for a fuel stop. As soon as we were refueled, my plan was to fly one more hour north to my airbase at Lubero in the Kivu mountains and spend the Sabbath with my family and show the passengers our part of the world. I had plenty of time, and the flight to Nairobi wouldn't happen until later

anyway. As I descended into Goma, I buzzed the northeastern Zaire mission headquarters and then landed. We waited for the mission truck to bring a drum of aviation gasoline to us. Soon the plane was refueled, and we were ready to head home.

However, when I tried to start the engine, the starter would not even rotate the propeller. There must be a problem with the starter, I figured, so I pulled off the starter and inspected it the best that I could with the available tools. I laid the starter onto the engine for a "ground," but when I hit the starter switch, it would barely rotate the drive spline. While I was working, a pilot friend who was flying in the area suggested a new set of brushes and loaned a set to me when he landed, but the result was still no rotation. I tried to hand-prop start the engine, but that also did not work.

So, I called my wife on the radio and told her that we would be spending the Sabbath in Goma instead. We spent the day worshiping and fellowshiping with the staff and church family there.

Next morning, I worked on the starter for some time. But time was slipping away, so the passengers and I climbed into the plane. We bowed our heads, and I prayed, "Lord, if it is

Your will that this family catch their flight out of Nairobi tonight, You are going to have to start the engine." We all said, "Amen," and then I hit the starter switch and the engine came to life after only one revolution of the propeller.

I thanked God for personally starting the engine.

We were soon taking off out across the beautiful blue Lake Kivu, heading southeast to the Rwanda-Burundi border, and then we flew east along the border until we entered Tanzania and skirted along the southern shore of Lake Victoria. We landed at the Mwanza airport to top off the fuel tanks.

Our engine was hot now from flying for a couple of hours. When I tried to restart, again the engine would not start. So once again we bowed our heads, prayed the same prayer, and God answered it with the same result: it whirled to life after only one revolution. "Thank You, Lord."

Our flight to Nairobi was gorgeous: flying near Lake Victoria, enjoying the scenery of the famous Serengeti National Game Park, and finally crossing the Great Rift Valley just before we landed at the Wilson Airport (for small aircraft) in Nairobi.

After taxiing to the customs and immigration office, I stopped the engine, let the passengers out, and took care of the immigration process. Then, while they waited in a designated place, I tried to start the engine in order to taxi the plane down to my friend Alan Street's maintenance facilities. He was going to put our Cessna 185 in his shop for the night. However, you guessed it: it wouldn't start. I had to push it about one hundred yards along the apron, then park it.

Later that night the passengers were able to connect with their flight. God had helped us. But I still did not know why the plane had refused to start.

Monday morning, I drove out to the shop and again took off the starter. Now I had the special tools that I needed and completely disassembled it. During the process, I discovered that the field winding had welded itself to the starter case for about a half to three-fourths of an inch. Now I understood the problem: it was shorted out and *could not start.*

When Alan Street saw what I had found, he said, "There was absolutely no way *that* starter could have started the engine and that was *not* a recent weld." When I told him that the engine had started twice yesterday, his response was, "Not even possible."

God is so good. ❧

*T*he airliner had been flying in circles for a long time, and the pilot was desperate. Unless he found a flat open space in the dense jungle within five minutes, he and the passengers were all but doomed.

But the missionary kept praying.

This story really resonates with me since, in my boyhood as a missionary child in Latin America, we flew in planes similar to the one in this story—planes that were incapable of flying high enough to escape storms. From beginning to end, this story is one long interconnected miracle.

Jungle Landing

George Alden Thompson

The pilot was now circling our ship over the meandering, swollen river. The motors had been spitting for some little time. Surely it could not be long now before we would crash into the Colombian jungle. With so little gasoline there could not be much of an explosion when we hit, I assured myself.

We had terminated a pleasant two-week vacation in Bogotá. We were to leave the airport at 6:45 A.M. Friday for the fifty-minute flight to our mission home in Medellín. Though it had been difficult to get the children ready at such an early hour, we felt we could be better prepared for the Sabbath by arriving home early.

When we arrived at the airport, it was very foggy and cold. The sun had just begun to rise, but it did not penetrate the clouds.

We waited for some time, but the fog did not lift fast. We wondered whether we would be able to go as planned.

Shortly the call came for passengers to Medellín to line up. As the names were read, ours did not appear on the list. Upon questioning, I was told that this plane, No. 107, went to Medellín with passengers for Balboa, Canal Zone. We were scheduled for plane No. 102. In about fifteen minutes the passengers for that plane were called, and we happily boarded the ship. The stewardess greeted us, and we went to our seats.

The plane was a two-motor Douglas with only one row of seats on each side—space for fourteen passengers. Georgene, our five-year-old girl, sat across from me, and Lola, my wife, sat in front of Georgene with Alden, our two-year-old boy, on her lap. There were four other passengers: a man behind me, a girl of fifteen, a boy of seventeen, and a young woman who was dressed in mourning attire—very thin-faced and sad looking.

Once in the air, we could not see anything below, for we were between two layers of clouds. The ride was not very smooth because of the stormy conditions. The woman behind Georgene was quiet and began to show signs of sickness. Lola, too, began to feel nauseous. Alden would not stay with me for long—and wanted to be with his mother.

I was so bundled up that I couldn't get out my pocketwatch, so I asked Lola the time. I figured that in fifteen or twenty minutes we would land.

Soon that time passed. Though no one could see, I felt we must be circling over

Medellín. It is difficult to enter this city by plane, because it is set in a small valley between high mountains. We circled for some time, and I lost all sense of orientation. It was extremely cold. (We learned later that we were up as high as fourteen thousand feet.) It was stormy outside, and the clouds below us were exceedingly dense. Now and then we could catch a brief glimpse of land, but it clearly was not Medellín. The time was lengthening, and we were nervous.

The pilot was flying over mountainous country, and the plane was tossing considerably. Lola used the paper sack several times, and Georgene was beginning to complain of her "tummy" hurting. At first I thought we were going back to Bogotá, but soon realized that could not be, for it didn't look like Bogotá country.

The man behind me, Mr. Grey, asked what time it was. Lola answered, and then I told him that it generally took only fifty minutes for the trip to Medellín and that I felt we must be lost. The pilot was now flying close to the mountains and apparently was trying to follow a river. I thought maybe he was going to the coast city of Barranquilla and that surely we would soon come out of the storm. But far from that—it began to rain hard. The plane was going up and down among the hills, then close to the river. The voyage was very rough.

Georgene began to cry and said, "Daddy, I think this plane is going to land on a mountain." I reached over and patted her hand, and smilingly told her that Jesus would help us, and that we should pray. I looked back and smiled at the stewardess. She had fear written vividly on her face. Mr. Grey was very nervous. When he asked about the trip again, I told him I felt that only God could save us. I was certain we were lost and that the pilot did not know how to get out.

We now were flying closer to the river. The rain was falling in sheets. We were making sharp banks, rapid dives, and short circles. Apparently, the pilot was looking for a sand bar in the river upon which to make an emergency landing. The ride was fearful!

We could see the river quite frequently now, and we felt hot and steamy. Georgene was still whimpering. Mr. Grey was extremely nervous. Lola announced that we had been in the air more than two and a half hours. I felt queasy; I leaned back in my chair and tried to relax and breathe deeply. I cannot describe the plane's actions at that time for I was praying for the pilot.

I told Georgene to put on her seat belt, for I knew we must be running out of gas and would have to land somewhere.

She said, "Daddy, it doesn't say to put on our seat belts yet."

I told her to do it anyway and gave no reason. (The signal for all to use the safety belts was flashed on just a few minutes later.)

We were over dense tropical jungle. I looked back again and smiled at the stewardess. Her face was flushed—the picture of despair and nervousness. I had been singing softly and had thought much. I told Lola, "If God wants us to stop our work now, His will be done; but if He wants us to continue, He will save us."

Lola, though nervous, gave me a sweet and courageous answer, "I know it, dear." God bless her for her companionship and fortitude! We were now resigned to the Lord's will, and were calm, much less fearful than a while before.

The plane made a rapid dive, and I felt we would surely crash. We could see the river below now, and then as we dashed between the clouds, there was no place to land! The hills and canyons were rugged and covered with dense jungle. We were still circling, climbing, diving—going at a frightening speed—and still no place to land. I was praying for the pilot, I prayed for my wife and little children, I prayed for the passengers, I prayed for the school at Medellín, and I prayed for myself, for I had had a good look at George Thompson during those interminably frightful hours. I felt, however, that God would help us, and I sang some more.

It could not be long now. I leaned the chair back as far as I could to break the force of an impact slightly. Taking off my glasses, I told Lola to take hers off, as well. I said, "We will have to make a forced landing." Alden was sleeping on her lap, and we decided not to awaken him.

It was still raining—the clouds were dispersing a little, and the heat was suffocating. As the pilot made a sharp bank over the river, I saw a small island. It was densely covered with vegetation except on one side, where it was a little barren and quite level. Was it long enough to land on?

The plane made an extremely sharp bank over the river close to the island. The wing almost touched the water. The plane righted itself—the hills were close upon us and maneuvering was very difficult. We circled again, and I knew the pilot was going to try to land on that small island. We made a wide circle this time and then headed up the river. We were close to the treetops and descending rapidly.

The emergency bell in the cabin rang for the stewardess. I looked back at her. The poor girl was frantic—did not know what to do. The young man told her to go answer, and I nodded assent. She opened the cabin door and steam rolled out. She got the message, slammed the door, sat in the first front seat, and tightened her belt. We were calm in the thought that God could save us if He so willed.

The plane leveled over the water. We hit the island with a tremendous crash, swerving wildly and scraping the rocks. Beyond was the raging river. The plane swerved to the right and suddenly stopped. It was 10:15 A.M.

I was too filled with emotion and praise to speak. We had not been badly jarred, and no one was scratched. The pilot did not use the landing gear for fear of soft mud, so we landed belly first. If the soil had been softer, we would probably have had our heads snapped off; and if it had been harder, the propellers would not have served as brakes but would have snapped, and we would have gone into the river on the other side of the island. The pilot was tops! God had guided him, and we were safe. We had landed along the very edge of the island, with the left wing out over the water.

The copilot came out with the captain and radioman. The captain said, "We are awfully sorry. All is OK. Just stay where you are." They then went outside to look over the plane. I said to the passengers, "It is only a miracle of God that we were saved. Let us kneel down right here and thank Him." The crew had returned, and I asked the captain to join us.

He said, "No. We got along all right. This was planned."

I felt sorry but did not press the matter. I then went to my wife quietly and kissed her and thanked God for deliverance. We made a fervent pledge to rededicate our all to the finishing of His work.

As I looked to the rear of the plane, I saw a small group of passengers kneeling and saying their prayers. Mr. Grey was listening reverently, so I said to him, "I do not know to what faith you belong, but we would like to have you kneel with us while we pray." He whispered, "I'm a Mason." We knelt, and I offered a short prayer of thanksgiving.

In a few minutes, some Indian men approached us in canoes hollowed out of logs. Soon another came and told us we must get out at once because the river was fierce and rising rapidly. In about fifteen minutes, the water had surrounded the plane. Our landing had been made in the nick of time! So we left the ship, boarded the canoes, and went about a half mile up the river to a little mining camp. We were greeted kindly by more young men and some Colombian miners.

Word had come by radio that launches from the big mining camp farther up the river would come soon and take us to the Pacific port city of Buenaventura. It was now close to noon. We were not sure of immediate rescue, but were told that a hydroplane would come and pick us up. That was good news. However, one of the miners said it was impossible for a hydroplane to make a landing on such a rough river.

About three o'clock we heard a plane, and sure enough, it was scouting our position. It was a land plane. It dropped supplies of food by parachute, saluted us after circling several times, and continued on its way. Shortly afterward, two motor launches arrived to take us to the large camp. The three-hour ride up the San Juan River to that camp was indeed thrilling. The water had risen eighteen feet at the upper camp, above normal bounds, and was a seething torrent in many places. Some of the huts bordering the river, though built upon stilts, already had water covering their floors.

The jungle was most interesting to us. As we saw the heavy growth of vegetation along the river, we were indeed thankful we'd not landed back in the mountains, for it would have been impossible to walk in that jungle! Truly the Lord had guided our pilot to the only place in all that vast region upon which to make a safe emergency landing.

He told us he had circled Medellín for

twenty minutes. Plane No. 107 was fifteen minutes ahead of us and had made a safe landing, but as our captain waited for the all-clear on the field, the fog completely concealed the valley from his view. After trying unsuccessfully to find two emergency landing fields, which were obscured by the fog, he finally radioed, "Have gas for five more minutes. Will land wherever I can." We believe it was indeed a miracle that a safe landing was made under such circumstances.

The next morning after breakfast we called our children to join in morning worship. Lola had been reading Psalm 34. When she handed the Bible to me, my eyes caught some verses in Psalm 36, and I selected it for reading. In verse 5, we saw the answer to our prayers: "Thy mercy, O Lord, is in the heavens; and thy faithfulness reacheth into the clouds." I stopped. Praise God for His mercy and His faithfulness! ❧

*T*he economy of post–World War I Germany was in shambles, and the German mark was worth almost nothing.

As for the missionary seminary, without enough hard currency to buy coal for the winter, it seemed they had no alternative but to close the school.

Well, there was one possibility, but it was so laughably improbable—why even try?

Even though the events in this story appear so improbable as to be ridiculous, they don't seem so to me. Reason being this: my missionary father had faith just as absolute as that evidenced by Pastor Vitins.

MIRACLE IN MAGDEBURG

Paul K. Freiwirth

"We serve a living God, who can still do great wonders," declared Pastor Wilhelm Vitins, business manager of the training school in Friedensau, Germany. It was an August evening in 1923, almost five years after the close of the First World War, and he had just returned from a trip to nearby Magdeburg. It took just such a God to save Friedensau in the greatest crisis of its history. Inflation's ghastly arm was threatening to disrupt the work of God in postwar Germany. Friedensau (Meadow of Peace), which had been training stalwart workers for Germany and many far-flung mission fields for almost twenty-five years, seemed to be the next victim. Inflation and education were about as easy to mix as oil and water.

The German mark was fluctuating more than a dozen times daily. In the early days of inflation, it had taken anywhere from ten million to fifty million marks to buy a dollar, all depending upon countless unpredictable and uncontrollable circumstances. Later on, in its dying throes, when the mark was hitting rock bottom at ten trillion to the dollar, a weary populace were talking about the *gallopierende Schwindsucht* (galloping consumption) of their worthless currency.

Friedensau's enrollment stood at two hundred in 1923. The various industries on the campus were providing employment for the students as well as for forty-five residents of the village. As the economic turmoil continued to grow, it became necessary to dismiss all non-student help, to sell two locomobiles as well as other vital equipment, and to enforce a set of stringent economy measures. Under the continued blessing of God, the school began to prosper and even became self-supporting for the first time in its history, while other institutions all around were reeling hopelessly under the staggering burden of inflation.

One day, however, a dreadful discovery was made: There would be no coal for the coming school year! The French Army of Occupation in the Ruhr was demanding priority, and supplies were dwindling at an alarming rate all over the country. Friedensau would be left high and dry, and it looked as though the school would be forced to close down.

It was with very heavy hearts that those in charge decided to hold a board meeting. Everyone knew what the outcome would be, and gloom settled over the beautiful campus as faculty and students thought of the great blow the work of God was to receive. Friedensau had been the pride of the constituency of the Central European Division, and only the books of heaven contained a true report of the institution's noble and far-reaching influence.

Conspicuous by his absence at this deliberation was the business manager, who until very recently had been engaged in successful evangelism in the Baltic countries. The impending end of Friedensau was haunting him day and night. After much earnest wrestling with God and with a prayer in his heart, he had left the campus very early that morning for Magdeburg, and when he arrived he visited one of the banks in that city.

With his faith in the overruling providence of God, Pastor Vitins had brought his last American money: five hundred dollars. He knew full well that he could get coal for every cent of this much-sought-after currency, but there was one great snag in his scheme: At the rate of exchange, which had been surprisingly stable during the last fortnight, it would take exactly ten times as many dollars as he had to purchase a year's coal supply for Friedensau. Before this could be possible, the mark would have to drop to one-tenth of its value, and there was no earthly indication that this was going to take place within the foreseeable future, much less before the evening of this day.

But then why not? thought Pastor Vitins. He remembered having preached on how the Lord helped Elisha to bring the borrowed iron ax to the surface of the water into which it had been dropped, thus saving an ancient school of the prophets from embarrassment and loss.

Could not the same God who made the iron ax come to the surface send the mark more deeply into the bottom of inflation's maddening maelstrom to save a school of the prophets in 1923? Had He not said that "the silver is mine, and the gold is mine" [Haggai 2:8], and was not this ludicrously inadequate emergency money of earth's last hour also under His control?

Promptly at nine o'clock, Pastor Vitins flashed the greenbacks under the eager eyes of one of the bank's tellers. The exchange rate of the previous day was offered him.

"I'll try again later," was his polite response.

After the longest sixty minutes in his life, Pastor Vitins approached the teller again.

"The mark has fallen 50 percent; will you sell now?" the teller said.

"Sorry, not interested," replied Pastor Vitins, "I'll wait till the dollar stands ten times above yesterday's rate." The teller told his preacher friend that his hope was foolhardy, but to his great disappointment, here was one fool who could not be parted from his money easily!

After forty-five minutes more, the dollar stood at six times the previous day's exchange. The mark had hit Skid Row all right, and the great question was, How long would it skid, and why was it skidding just today, and so much? Only God's servant knew why, and he continued to refuse to sell. The dollar was rising steadily all morning. The teller tried several times to buy Pastor Vitins's five hundred dollars, but every effort was met with the same reply: "I'm waiting till the rate is ten times as favorable as it was yesterday."

The fingers of the venerable clock showed ten minutes to twelve, and the dollar was nine and a half times above yesterday's rate. The frantic teller all but got down on his shaky knees. Then came 11:55 A.M. *Flash!* The exchange rate was actually ten times as favorable as yesterday! Now our brother eagerly offered his dollars, and the teller as eagerly gave his signature. By long-distance telephone, the coal was ordered at the rate of exchange of that very minute. Friedensau was saved! The noon recess came, and all business stopped for an hour.

Pastor Vitins did not know whether to be exhausted, to be thankful, or to pinch himself to make sure that he was not dreaming. The greatest surprise was yet to come though! Out of sheer human curiosity, the happy business manager decided to observe the fluctuations during the afternoon. To be sure, the mark was climbing again, quickly and steadily, to where it had stood the day before. Speculators were disappointed, and regretted not having sold when the dollar had reached the day's peak at 11:55 A.M. A careful survey of all Germany later showed that *the only transaction made anywhere at that rate had been made by Friedensau's business manager to save his beloved school from an otherwise inevitable fate!* Inflation's wild juggernaut, the very thing the enemy of God was going to use to close Friedensau, had miraculously saved it from impending doom! "Surely the wrath of man shall praise thee: the remainder of wrath shalt thou restrain" [Psalm 76:10].

Was ever a gloomier day followed by a happier evening? As soon as Pastor Vitins arrived from Magdeburg with the good news, the decision of the school board was reversed, and immediate plans for a school year began to be made. The regular evening worship was turned into a praise and testimony service, the like of which Friedensau had never before witnessed.

Almost immediately the coal began to arrive. Each wagonload impressed upon the hearts of the students the signal providence of God anew. With the fervent prayer of thankfulness for the coal from Magdeburg there was awakened a new and deeper yearning for the blessing of the live coal from off the altar of heaven which, given to Isaiah, touched his lips and transformed his life. And as one man, there reverberated from Friedensau's hallowed halls the same answer given by the gospel prophet in response to Heaven's call, "For whom shall I send, and who will go for me?"

"Here am I; send me" [Isaiah 6:8]. ❧

*I*t was an uneventful day that didn't stay that way. Life—or death—which would it be?

Since I was only a boy when these events took place, I just accepted them as commonplace. Only now, over half a century later, do I realize how miraculous they really were.

REVOLUTION!

Joseph Leininger Wheeler

It was a calm and beautiful day in Guatemala City, and I was browsing in one of my favorite haunts: the American library. Suddenly we heard a commotion outside, and someone ran into the reading room, shouting, *"Revolución! Revolución!"*

He was followed by the head librarian, who told us that there was no time to waste: each one of us should get out and get home as fast as possible, as already there was shooting in the streets. Then he commanded us to leave *immediately*!

We did, but I, being a typical "invincible" thirteen-year-old boy, with a severe shortage of common sense, excitedly mounted my heavy blue bicycle and raced off toward the National Palace to check out the action—the very *last* place I should have been in a revolution! As I reached the plaza, a stern-looking policeman stopped me and barked out, "You stupid gringo kid, don't you know there's a revolution on? Get home fast! You're lucky you're not dead!"

Only then did I head home, but I was undeniably crestfallen that I was missing all the excitement. As I rode through street after street, I saw long lines of women and children queueing up outside the *tiendas* (small grocery stores). I stopped to ask one of the people in line what they were doing and why. The answer: "Don't you know there's a revolution on?"

"Yes . . . *so?*"

Then I was informed that some revolutions happened quickly; others lasted a long time. This one appeared to be one of those that wouldn't end soon. So everyone was stocking up on food before fighting spread into the streets.

So, home I went. My mother, who feared for my safety, was deeply relieved to see me. When I told her what I'd seen and heard, she quickly wrote out a list of food items we'd need—especially those Latin American staples: rice and beans—then all but pushed me out the door, urging me to hurry!

Soon I, too, was standing in line, my coin purse safety-pinned to the inside of my right front pocket. I listened intently to what my neighbors were saying about what they'd heard about the revolution. Turns out that the leading general had become too popular for his own good. Indeed, the president had given him an assignment requiring him to board a military DC-3 and fly to a certain city in the interior. When the plane landed there and he emerged and descended the portable stairway, he was machine-gunned down. *That's* what the revolution was all about.

After purchasing my rice and beans and other items, I reluctantly returned home. Inside our house, Mom was already beginning to move furniture. After consulting with other nearby missionaries, they'd unilaterally concluded that they'd each better barricade their front doors and streetside barred windows. As for my father, I knew he was somewhere in the interior of the country inspecting church schools with the president of the Adventist mission, Melvin Sickler. All communication with the two men had ceased, so no one knew whether they were dead or alive. So, with her voice quavering, Mom told me, "Joey, until Dad returns, *you're* the man of the house. Help me move the tallest and heaviest furniture to the street side of the house, in order to barricade us from those who'll soon be fighting each other in the streets."

Thus Mom and I, and seven-year-old Romayne, strained our utmost to move our heavy mahogany armoires from the bedrooms to the street side of the house. It took us a long time because we also had to barricade the garage door—a door to a garage that housed only storage stuff, because we had no car of our own.

Finally, we had done all that was in our power to protect ourselves. The rest was up to God. Mom led us in the first of almost continual prayers that Dad and Elder Sickler's lives would be spared, wherever they might be.

I couldn't help asking, "Isn't Dad returning home tonight?"

Mom's face blanched. "*Y–e–s,* he and Elder Sickler are *supposed* to be returning tonight—or tomorrow."

"So," I continued, "if he *does,* how's he going to get into our house, since we've barricaded the front door?"

"We'll face that if—or when—we hear him trying to get in."

(Back then, in the late 1940s, missionaries like us had no telephone; the nearest one being in the mission office.)

A Close Call

And so began the long waiting game, punctuated by near-constant gunfire in the streets, periodic nearby explosions, the boom of big guns, and the whine of shells. There were two large forts on opposite sides of the city, one held by rebels loyal to the slain general's cause, and the other controlled by forces loyal to the president. Every so many minutes, day and night, we would hear the boom of one of those great guns, followed by the whine as the shells passed over our home, and the sound made by the detonating shell as it reached its target. Yes, almost unbelievably, we had ringside seats between the two forts. And the sounds were anything but muffled because we had an open patio in the middle of the house.

Hour after hour passed, with rarely ever a moment of silence. It became increasingly difficult for me to concentrate on my lessons. Marooned in the house as we were, I began to go stir-crazy. All that action outside and above—and me unable to see a thing.

Finally, I could stand it no longer: I walked over to the base of the concrete stairway that led from the patio to the roof terrace where Mom dried our clothes and surreptitiously looked around to make sure Mom wasn't watching me, for we'd been warned not to go upstairs until the revolution was over. Then I sneaked up the stairway to the roof. *Now,* finally, I'd be able to watch the action and see how a revolution worked.

Just as I stepped onto the terrace, there was a boom and then, almost simultaneously, the unbelievably close whine of a shell—but the shell reached me before the whine: it came so close I was almost deafened. But what sent chills up my spine was that it was so close—it couldn't have missed my head by more than inches—I felt the hot wind of its passing. So close that all these years later I can still feel that displacement of air. Indeed, I was in such shock that I can't even remember how I descended to the patio.

Knowing what Mom would have said to me if she'd known of my disobedient act, I didn't tell her what I'd done. Not until many years later, when I'd grown up and felt safe from parental retribution, did I inform her of my wrongdoing.

Stuck in a Mudhole

Meanwhile, as the hours, days, and nights slowly passed, our prayer vigil for Dad and Elder Sickler continued. The strain on Mom was really taking its toll. Since we were cut off even from the other missionaries, minutes seemed like hours, hours like days, and days like weeks.

Finally, there was a loud pounding on our front door. When Mom fearfully asked who it was (in Spanish, of course), there came the heavenly sound of Dad's voice, asking to be let in.

Oh what an ecstasy of furniture moving followed! Once Dad was restored to us, everyone talked at once. So much so that Baby Marjorie started to cry.

Eventually things calmed down enough for Dad to tell his story: Yes, he and Elder Sickler were heading back in the mission Jeep to Guatemala City the evening the revolution began. News of the revolution hadn't yet reached that part of the country. But suddenly, they were engulfed by torrential rain—rain that didn't reach us in the capital at all. Once begun, the storm continued unabated. The dirt road soon flooded; the flooded road became a lake, and the Jeep sank deeper and deeper into the muck until the engine was powerless to move it forward or backward. So there they were stuck—alone. Hour after hour passed, and they kept praying that God would send help so they could make it home.

Three days later, the rain stopped and a truck drove into sight! After some time and much effort, the Jeep was winched out of its mud hole. Only then did they learn of the revolution, which had finally begun to ebb.

So, belatedly, they resumed their journey toward the capital. They were stopped many times at check stations along the way. One official declared that someone must have been watching out for them, for in the early days of the revolution, the soldiers were shooting first and asking questions afterward. And they in a military-looking Jeep! They'd *never* have made it into the city alive!

What a string of miracles! Saving my life twice (once at the National Palace plaza and later on the terrace of our home) and saving the lives of my father and Elder Sickler by sending such a continuous downpour that they were powerless to move for three long days.

Clearly, God's plans for my life and my father's life were not yet complete. We both still had unfinished business before us. ❧

SECTION FOUR

"Whatever you decide to do will be accomplished,
and light will shine on the road ahead of you."
Job 22:28 (NLT)

Not just in mission lands do God's angels intervene against angry mobs, but in supposedly civilized lands as well. Miraculously, Dr. Adam Clarke, author of Clarke's commentary, thanks to the protection of God's angels, made it through unscathed time after time—just as happened when Christ was assailed by mobs prior to the Crucifixion.

When I was young, I devoured such missionary accounts as these, thus they made a lasting impact on my life. However, I can't help wondering whether such family reading material gets into Christian homes much anymore.

AN ANGRY MOB HELD POWERLESS

Adam Clarke

As a Methodist pioneer, Dr. Adam Clarke, of Ireland, author of the "Commentary," traveled all about Ireland, England, and Wales, and to the Channel Islands. In those days, Methodism met the opposition of the Established Church and of "society," and the irreligious mob felt itself doing respectable service in assailing the sect everywhere spoken against.

On one of those trips, Dr. Clarke experienced so remarkable an interposition of Providence to save his life that he records it in his commentary, as a note on the deliverance of Christ from the mob at Nazareth (Luke 4:30). Writing of himself in the third person, he says a certain missionary was called to preach in a place where there was much prejudice:

"About fifty people who had received impressions from the Word of God assembled. He began his discourse, and after he had preached about thirty minutes, a furious mob surrounded the house, armed with different instruments of death, and breathing the most sanguinary threats. Some who were within closed the door; and the missionary and his flock prayed to God for help.

"The mob assailed the house, and began to hurl stones against the walls, windows, and roof; and in a short time almost every tile was destroyed, and the roof nearly uncovered, and before they quitted the premises, scarcely left one square inch of glass in its five windows.

"While this was going forward, a person came with a pistol to the window opposite to the place where the preacher stood (who was then exhorting his flock to be steady, to resign themselves to God, and trust in Him), aimed it at him, and snapped it, but it only flashed in the pan.

"As the house was a wooden building, the mob began with crowbars and shovels to undermine it, and take away its principal supports. The preacher then addressed his little flock to this effect: 'These attackers seek not you, but me; if I continue in the house, they will soon tear it down, and we shall all be buried in the ruins; I will therefore, in the name of God, go out to them, and you will be safe.' He then went toward the door; but the assailed people surrounded him and urged him not to venture out, as he might expect to be instantly massacred. Nevertheless, he went calmly forward, opened the door, at which a whole volley of stones and dirt was that instant discharged; but he received no wounds.

"There were so many people in the mob that there seemed no possible way for him to escape. As soon as the preacher made his appearance, the savage attackers became instantly as silent and as still as night; as he walked forward, they divided to the right and to the left, leaving a passage of about four feet wide, for himself and a young man who followed him to walk in. He passed on through the whole crowd, not a soul of whom either lifted a hand or spoke one word, till he and his companion had gained the uttermost skirts of the mob. The narrator, who was present on the occasion, goes on to say:

" 'This was one of the most affecting spectacles I ever witnessed: an infuriated mob without any visible cause (for the preacher spoke not one word) became in a moment as calm as lambs. They seemed struck with amazement bordering on stupefaction; they stared and stood speechless; and after they had fallen back to right and left to leave him a free passage, they were as motionless as statues. They had assembled with the full purpose of killing the man who came to show them the way of salvation; but he, passing through the midst of them, escaped without a blow being struck. Was not the God of missionaries in this work?' "

In the quietness that followed for a few minutes after the preacher disappeared, the people inside the church also walked out and escaped. Then the mob awoke "as from a dream," and broke the windows and otherwise vented their fury on the house.

The One who, passing through the midst of the mob at Nazareth, also went on His way, has promised the gospel worker, "Lo, I am with you alway, even unto the end of the world" [Matthew 28:20]. ❧

*H*udson Taylor, the founder of the China Inland Mission, tells the remarkable story of Wang in these words.

Wang, of Hosi, in Chekiang, was called to begin his search for the light of life in an evidently providential way.

This particular story challenges a long-held assumption of mine: that unless Christian missionaries were proactive in rescuing non-Christians, conversions would not take place. Not until I read this Hudson Taylor story did I realize that God Himself can be proactive and initiate the conversion process.

How Wang Was Called Into the Light

Hudson Taylor

Old Wang was a farmer, whose subsequent life of devotion and soul winning in his community set the seal of genuineness upon his experience. He was brought to Hudson Taylor in Ningpo by a Chinese evangelist who had met the man in a tea shop. As soon as Wang heard the evangelist speak of Christianity, he went to him and said, "I want to learn more of this strange religion." So he was brought to Mr. Taylor:

"It was a strange story he told us, one to which at that time we scarcely gave credence.

"Some six or seven months before, he had been very ill; everyone thought him at the point of death. One day he was left alone in the house, all his family being out at work, when he distinctly heard himself called by name. Wide awake, and perfectly conscious, he looked around for the speaker, but saw no one. Feeling very uncomfortable, he got out of bed, and unable from weakness to cross the room, crept to the door by the help of furniture and walls. But on looking out he was even more perplexed, for still there was no one to be seen. Back into bed again he crept, wondering if he could have been mistaken, when he heard the voice a second time. Again he crawled out to the door. Again, no one. Alarmed, he feebly made his way back, and buried his face beneath the coverlet, now thinking that the voice he heard must be the summons of death, and dreading to see some hideous apparition come to drag away his spirit, he knew not whither.

"Instead of this, however, he heard the voice a third time, and it went on quietly to direct him to make an infusion of some simple herb that would cure his complaint, and to go, upon recovery, to the city of Ningpo, where he would learn of a new religion which he was to follow.

"When the family came home, he got someone to make him the herb tea, by the use of which he speedily recovered; and when strengthened, he came to Ningpo. Having no other method of obtaining a livelihood, he supported himself as a grasscutter.

"He had been thus employed in the city, but had never heard the gospel. As soon as he met with Neng-kuei, however, in the tea shop, he concluded that this must be the new religion he had been directed to seek."

At first the missionaries thought the inquirer, with so remarkable a story, must have some mercenary purpose; but his life convinced all that the Lord had truly called the old man out of darkness into light. He was firmly established in the faith of the gospel, and when visited at his home some years later, a company of believers was found, raised up by the farmer's godly life and teaching. ❧

*T*he legendary missionary John G. Paton landed on the island of Tanna in the New Hebrides in the year 1858, having been sent there by the Reformed Presbyterian Church of Scotland. Miraculously, he survived numerous attempts on his life.

Fortunately for posterity, Mr. Paton kept a journal, which chronicled a world that no longer exists, a world of headhunters, cannibals, and barbarism—yet also a world of loyalty, trustworthiness, and kindness.

This particular story Paton wrote down, as it happened, in his journal. It is not "politically correct" for us today, for it was written in the colonial world of almost a century and a half ago. Nevertheless, it remains deeply moving, for it reveals how total Paton's commitment was, both to the people he ministered to and to the God he represented. And how great was his faith.

I found this to be one of the most fascinating missionary stories I have ever read. Mainly because it portrays non-Christian natives not as the usual pots missionaries pour Christianity into but rather as being surprisingly equal in intelligence, awareness, and capacity to grow from observation and experience—on their own!

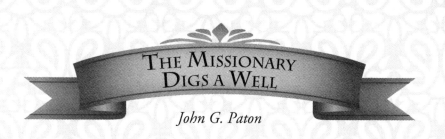

Aniwa being a flat coral island, with no hills to attract the clouds, rain is scarce there as compared with the adjoining mountainous islands; and even when it does fall heavily, with tropical profusion, it disappears through the light soil and porous rock, and drains itself directly into the sea. The rainy season is from December to April, and then the disease most characteristic of all these regions is apt to prevail: fever and ague.

At certain seasons, the natives drink very unwholesome water; and, indeed, the best water they had at any time for drinking purposes was from the precious coconut, a kind of apple of Paradise for all these southern isles. They also cultivate the sugar cane very extensively, and in great variety; and they chew it, when we would fly to water for thirst; so it is to them both food and drink. The black fellow carries with him to the field, when he goes off for a day's work, four or five sticks of sugar cane, and puts in his time comfortably enough on these. Besides, the sea being their universal bathing place, in which they swattle [splash] like fish, and little water, almost none, being required for cooking purposes, and none whatever for washing clothes, the lack of fresh-springing water was not the dreadful trial to

them that it would be to us. Yet they appreciate and rejoice in it immensely, too; though the water of the green coconut is refreshing, and in appearance, taste, and color not unlike lemonade—one nut filling a tumbler; and though when mothers die they feed the babies on it and on the soft white pith, and they flourish on the same, yet the natives themselves show their delight in preferring, when they can get it, the water from the well.

Aniwa, having therefore no permanent supply of fresh water, in spring or stream or lake, and my own household also suffering sadly for lack of the same, I resolved by the help of God to sink a well near the mission premises, hoping that a wisdom higher than my own would guide me to the source of some blessed spring. Of the scientific conditions of such an experiment I was comparatively ignorant; but I counted on having to dig through earth and coral over thirty feet, and my constant fear was, that owing to our environment, the water, if water I found, would only be salt water, after all my toils! Still I resolved to sink that shaft in hope, and in faith that the Son of God would be glorified thereby.

One morning I said to the old chief and his fellow chief, both now earnestly inquiring about the religion of Jehovah and of Jesus, "I am going to sink a deep well down into the earth, to see if our God will send us fresh water up from below."

They looked at me with astonishment, and said in a tone of sympathy approaching pity, "O Missi! Wait till the rain comes down, and we will save all we possibly can for you."

I replied, "We may all die for lack of water. If no fresh water can be got, we may be forced to leave you."

The old chief looked imploringly, and said, "O Missi! You must not leave us for that. Rain comes only from above. How could you expect our island to send up showers of rain from below?"

I told him, "Fresh water does come up springing from the earth in my land, and I hope to see it here also."

The old chief grew more tender in his tones and cried, "O Missi, your head is going wrong; you are losing something, or you would not talk wild like that! Don't let our people hear you talking about going down into the earth for rain, or they will never listen to your word or believe you again."

But I started upon my hazardous job, selecting a spot near the mission station and close to the public path, that my prospective well might be useful to all. I began to dig, with pick and spade and bucket at hand, an American ax for a hammer and crowbar, and a ladder for service by and by. The good old chief now sent his men in relays to watch me, lest I should attempt to take my own life, or do anything

outrageous, saying, "Poor Missi! That's the way with all who go mad. There's no driving of a notion out of their heads. We must just watch him now. He will find it harder to work with pick and spade than with his pen, and when he's tired, we'll persuade him to give it up."

I did get exhausted sooner than I expected, toiling under that tropical sun; but we never admit to the natives that we are beaten; so I went into the house and filled my vest pocket with large beautiful English-made fishhooks. These are very tempting to the young men as compared with their own, skillfully made though they be out of shell, and serving their purposes wonderfully. Holding up a large hook, I cried, "One of these to every man who fills and turns over three buckets out of this hole!"

A rush was made to get the first turn, and back again for another and another. I kept those on one side who had got a turn, till all the rest in order had a chance, and bucket after bucket was filled and emptied rapidly. Still the shaft seemed to lower very slowly, while my fishhooks were disappearing very quickly. I was constantly there, and took the heavy share of everything, and was thankful one evening to find that we had cleared more than twelve feet deep, when lo! next morning, one side had fallen in, and our work was all undone.

The old chief and his best men now came around me more earnestly than ever. He remonstrated with me very gravely. He assured me for the fiftieth time that rain would never be seen coming up through the earth on Aniwa.

"Now," he said, "had you been in that hole

last night you would have been buried, and a man-of-war would have come from Queen Toria [Victoria] to ask for the Missi that lived here. We would have to say, 'He is down in that hole.' The captain would ask, 'Who killed him and put him down there?' We would have to say, 'He went down there himself!' The captain would answer, 'Nonsense! Who ever heard of a white man's going down into the earth to bury himself? You killed him, you put him there; don't hide your bad conduct with lies!' Then he would bring out his big guns and shoot us, and destroy our island in revenge. You are making your own grave, Missi, and you will make ours too. Give up this mad freak, for no rain will be found by going downward on Aniwa. Besides, all your fishhooks cannot tempt my men again to enter that hole; they don't want to be buried with you. Will you not give it up now?"

I said all that I could to quiet his fears, explained to them that this falling in had happened by my neglect of precautions, and finally made known that by the help of my God, even without all other help, I meant to persevere.

Steeping my poor brains over the problem, I became an extemporized engineer. Two trees were searched for, with branches on opposite sides, capable of sustaining a cross tree betwixt them. I sank them on each side firmly into the ground, passed the beam across them over the center of the shaft, fastened thereon a rude homemade pulley and block, passed a rope over the wheel, and swung my largest bucket to the end of it. Thus equipped, I began once more sinking away at the well, but at so great an angle

that the sides might not again fall in. Not a native, however, would enter that hole, and I had to pick and dig away till I was utterly exhausted. But a native teacher, in whom I had confidence, took charge above, managing to hire them with axes, knives, etc., to seize the end of the rope and walk along the ground, pulling it till the bucket rose to the surface, and then he himself swung it aside, emptied it, and lowered it down again. I rang a little bell that I had with me when the bucket was loaded, and that was the signal for my brave helpers to pull their rope. And thus I toiled on from day to day, my heart almost sinking sometimes with the sinking of a well, till we reached a depth of about thirty feet. And the phrase, "living water," "living water," kept chiming through my soul like music from God, as I dug and hammered away!

At this depth the earth and coral began to be soaked with damp. I felt that we were nearing water. My soul had a faith that God would open a spring for us; but side by side with this faith was a strange terror that the water would be salt. So perplexing and mixed are even the highest experiences of the soul; the rose-flower of a perfect faith, set round and round with prickly thorns. One evening I said to the old chief, "I think that Jehovah God will give us water tomorrow from that hole!"

The chief said, "No, Missi; you will never see rain coming up from the earth on this island. We wonder what is to be the end of this mad work of yours. We expect daily, if you reach water, to see you drop through into the sea and the sharks will eat you! That will be the end of it; death to you, and danger to us all."

I still answered, "Come tomorrow. I believe that Jehovah God will send you the rain water up through the earth."

Next morning I went down again at daybreak, and sank a narrow hole in the center about two feet deep. The perspiration broke over me with uncontrollable excitement, and I trembled through every limb, when the water rushed up and began to fill the hole. Muddy though it was, I eagerly tasted it, lapping it with my trembling hand, and then I almost fell upon my knees in that muddy bottom as my heart burst up in praise to the Lord. It was water! It was fresh water. It was living water from Jehovah's well! True, it was a little brackish, but nothing to speak of; and no spring in the desert, cooling the parched lips of a fevered pilgrim, ever appeared more worthy of being called a well of God than did that water to me.

The chiefs had assembled with their men nearby. They waited on in eager expectancy. It was a rehearsal, in a small way, of the Israelites' coming round, while Moses struck the rock and called for water. By and by, when I had praised the Lord, and my excitement was a little calmed, the mud being also greatly settled, I filled a jug, which I had taken down empty in the sight of them all, and ascended to the top, called for them to come and see the rain which Jehovah God had given us through the well. They closed around me in haste, and gazed on it in superstitious fear. The old chief shook it to see if it would spill, and then touched it to see if it felt like water. At last he tasted it, and

rolling it in his mouth with joy for a moment, he swallowed it, and shouted, "Rain! Rain! Yes, it is rain! But how did you get it?"

I repeated, "Jehovah, my God, gave it out of His own earth in answer to our labors and prayers. Go and see it springing up for yourselves!"

Now, though every man there could climb the highest tree as swiftly and as fearlessly as a squirrel or an opossum, not one of them had courage to walk to the side and gaze down into that well. To them this was miraculous! But they were not without resource that met the emergency. They agreed to take firm hold of each other by the hand, to place themselves in a long line, the foremost man to lean cautiously forward, gaze into the well, and then pass to the rear, and so on till all had seen "Jehovah's rain" far below. It was somewhat comical, yet far more pathetic, to stand by and watch their faces, as man after man peered down into the mystery, and then looked up at me in blank bewilderment. When all had seen it with their very own eyes, and were "weak with wonder," the old chief exclaimed:

"Missi, wonderful, wonderful is the work of your Jehovah God! No god of Aniwa ever helped us in this way. The world is turned upside down since Jehovah came to Aniwa! But, Missi," continued he, after a pause that looked like silent worship, "will it always rain up through the earth? Or will it come and go like the rain from the clouds?"

I told them that I believed it would always continue there for our use, as a good gift from Jehovah.

"Well, but, Missi," replied the chief, some glimmering or self-interest beginning to strike his brain, "will you or your family drink it all, or shall we also have some?"

"You and all your people," I answered, "and all the people of the island, may come and drink and carry away as much of it as you wish. I believe there will always be plenty for us all, and the more of it we can use the fresher it will be. That is the way with many of our Jehovah's best gifts to men, and for it and for all we praise His name!"

"Then, Missi," said the chief, "it will be our water, and we may all use it as our very own."

"Yes," I answered, "whenever you wish it, and as much as you need, both here and at your own houses, as far as it can possibly be made to go."

The chief looked at me eagerly, fully convinced at last that the well contained a treasure, and exclaimed, "Missi, what can we do to help you now?"

I was thankful, indeed, to accept of the chief's assistance, now sorely needed, and I said, "You have seen it fall in once already. If it falls again, it will conceal the rain from below which our God has given us. In order to preserve it for us and for our children in all time, we must build it round and round with great coral blocks from the bottom to the very top. I will now clear it out, and prepare the foundation for this wall of coral. Let every man and woman carry from the shore the largest block they can bring. It is well worth all the toil thus to preserve our Jehovah's gift."

Scarcely were my words uttered, when they rushed to the shore, with shoutings and songs of gladness; and soon everyone was seen struggling under the biggest block of coral he dared to tackle. They lay like limestone rocks, broken up by the hurricanes, and rolled ashore in the arms of mighty billows; and in an incredibly short time scores of them were tumbled down for my use at the mouth of the well. Having prepared a foundation, I made ready a sort of bag-basket, into which every block was firmly tied and then let down to me by the pulley—a native teacher, a faithful fellow, cautiously guiding it. I received and placed each stone in its position, doing my poor best to wedge them one against the other, building circularly, and cutting them to the needed shape with my American ax. The wall is about three feet thick, and the masonry may be guaranteed to stand till the coral itself decays. I worked continuously, for fear of any further collapse, till I had it raised about twenty feet; and now, feeling secure, and my hands being dreadfully cut up, I intimated that I would rest a week or two, and finish the building then. But the chief advanced and said:

"Missi, you have been strong to work. Your strength has fled. But rest here beside us; and just point out where each block is to be laid. We will lay them there, we will build them solidly behind like you. And no man will sleep till it is done."

With all their will and heart they started on the job, some carrying, some cutting, and squaring the blocks, till the wall rose like magic, and a row of the hugest rocks laid round the top, bound all together, and formed the mouth of the well. Women, boys, and all wished to have a hand in building it, and it remains to this day, a solid wall of masonry, the circle being thirty-four feet deep, eight feet wide at the top, and six at the bottom. I floored it over with wood above all, and fixed the windlass and bucket, and there it stands as one of the greatest material blessings which the Lord has given to Aniwa.

Very strangely, though the natives themselves have since tried to sink six or seven wells in the most likely places near their different villages, they have either come to coral rock which they could not pierce, or found only water that was salt. And they say among themselves, "Missi not only used pick and spade, but he prayed and cried to his God. We have learned to dig, but not how to pray, and therefore Jehovah will not give us the rain from below!"

The well was now finished. The place was neatly fenced in. And the old chief said, "Missi, I think I could help you next Sabbath. Will you let me preach a sermon on the well?"

"Yes," I at once replied, "if you will try to bring all the people to hear you."

"Missi, I will try," he eagerly promised. The news spread like wildfire that the Chief Namakei was to be missionary on the next day for the worship, and the people, under great expectancy, urged each other to come and hear what he had to say.

Sabbath came round. Aniwa assembled in what was for that island a great crowd. Namakei appeared dressed in shirt and kilt. He was so excited, and flourished his tomahawk about at such a rate, that it was rather lively work to be near him. I conducted short opening devotions, and then called upon Namakei. He rose at once, with eye flashing wildly, and his limbs twitching with emotion. He spoke to the following effect, swinging his tomahawk to enforce every eloquent gesticulation:

"Friends of Namakei, men and women and children of Aniwa, listen to my words! Since Missi came here he has told many strange things we could not understand—things all too wonderful; and we said regarding many of them that they must be lies. White people might believe such nonsense, but we said that the black fellow knew better than to receive it. But of all his wonderful stories, we thought the strangest was about sinking down through the earth to get rain! Then we said to each other, The man's head is turned; he's gone mad. But the Missi prayed on and wrought on, telling us that Jehovah God heard and saw, and that his God would give him rain. Was he mad? Has he not got the rain deep down in the earth? We mocked at him; but the water was there all the same. We have laughed at other things which the Missi told us, because we could not see them. But from this day I believe that all he tells us about his Jehovah God is true. Someday our eyes will see it. For today we have seen the rain from the earth."

Then rising to a climax, first one foot and then the other making the broken coral on the floor fly behind like a war horse pawing the ground, he cried with great eloquence:

"My people, the people of Aniwa, the world is turned upside down since the word of Jehovah came to this land! Whoever expected to see rain coming up through the earth? It has always come from the clouds. Wonderful is the work of this Jehovah God. No god of Aniwa ever answered prayers as the Missi's God has done. Friends of Namakei, all the powers of the world could not have forced us to believe that rain could be given from the depths of the earth, if we had not seen it with our eyes, felt it, and tasted it as we here do. Now, by the help of Jehovah God the Missi brought that invisible rain to view, which we never before heard of or saw, and—" beating his hand on his breast, he exclaimed:

"Something here in my heart tells me that the Jehovah God does exist, the Invisible One, whom we never heard of nor saw till the Missi brought Him to our knowledge. The coral has been removed, the land has been cleared away, and lo! the water rises. Invisible till this day, yet all the same it was there, though our eyes were too weak. So I, your chief, do now firmly believe that one day I shall see the Invisible Jehovah God with my eyes, as Missi tells me, not less surely than I have seen the rain from the earth below. From this day, my people, I must worship the God who has opened for us the well, and who fills us with rain from below.

"The gods of Aniwa cannot hear, cannot help us, like the God of Missi. Henceforth I am a follower of Jehovah God. Let every man that thinks with me go now and fetch the idols of Aniwa, the gods which our fathers feared, and cast them down at Missi's feet. Let us burn and bury and destroy these things of wood and stone, and let us be taught by the Missi how to serve God who can hear, the Jehovah who gave us the well, and who will give us every other blessing, for He sent His Son Jesus to die for us and bring us to heaven. This is what the Missi has been telling us every day since he landed on Aniwa. We laughed at him, but now we believe him. The Jehovah God has sent us rain from the earth. Why should He not also send us His Son from heaven? Namakei stands up for Jehovah!"

This address, and the sinking of the well, broke the back of heathenism on Aniwa. That very afternoon, the old chief and several of his people brought their idols and cast them down at my feet beside the door of our house. Oh, the intense excitement of the weeks that followed! Company after company came to the spot, loaded with their gods of wood and stone, and piled them in heaps, amid the tears and sobs of some, and the shoutings of others, in which was heard the oft-repeated word, "Jehovah! Jehovah!" What could be burned, we cast into the flames; others we buried in pits twelve or fifteen feet deep; and some few, more likely than the rest to feed or awaken superstition, we sank far out into the deep sea. Heathen worship was gradually extinguished; and, though no one was compelled to come to church, every person on Aniwa, without exception, became ere many years an avowed worshiper of Jehovah God. Again,

"O Gallilean, Thou hast conquered!" ❧

*K*nowing of the threats against the young school teacher's life, the mayor urged her to henceforth carry a gun when venturing into the hills on errands of mercy.
But reading Psalm 121 convinced her to leave the pistol behind.
Little did she know . . .

Mary Markham's story makes me wonder: How often, when we carry guns for our own "protection," is it an admission that we don't trust God's guardian angels to protect us? Might not God assume by such decisions on our part that, rather than invade our will, He should leave us to our self-chosen course of action?

PROTECTED

Mary Markham

"Miss Jones, we feel that you would be safer on your trips in the hills if you would carry some means of protection. Just a little automatic—"

"But Mr. Davey, I never shot a pistol in my life! I'm afraid it wouldn't be a very good means of protection. I don't think anyone in these hills would be afraid of my bullets," laughed Miss Jones.

"I'll have one of the men take you down to the river, and you can practice there. We'd feel better if you would go armed hereafter. You know, without my telling you, that ever since the time when you found out about old Ma Kirk selling moonshine whisky for the Wilkins crowd, they have eyed you suspiciously. We greatly appreciate your work, and we don't intend to have anything happen to you if we can help it. All we ask is that you do a little cooperating."

"I am never afraid, Mr. Davey. I realize that since they know where I stand on the subject of temperance, there are some who wish I were out of the way, but I have never purposely provoked them. I don't deliberately try to find out what they are doing. That is not my work. My work is to teach my little school and help these folks the best I can."

"I know, Miss Jones. You're doing that well. There are some folks here who would give their lives for you, too; but there are others who would just as soon kill you as look at you, and you know it."

"Well, you're the mayor of this town, Mr. Davey, and I am willing to do anything you ask."

"Good. I'll have Monty take you down for a practice after school today. About four o'clock?"

At the appointed hour, Miss Jones was ready. She stood alone in the door of the little schoolhouse. Her eyes were very thoughtful as she looked toward the hills recently referred to in her talk with the mayor.

She had lived among the mountain people until she had learned to love them. Although her official capacity was teacher of the Echo Hollow School, she had become acquainted with these people through sickness and health, happiness and sorrow. No call for help had ever been unanswered. Those in need, be it physical or spiritual, had never been turned from her door. It was true that some of the practices which she observed were repulsive to her. And she did not hesitate, when the opportunity was ripe, to speak her convictions in no uncertain terms. Especially was this true when she felt that the lives and characters of her pupils were affected. In fact, her concern for the welfare of her pupils led to the incident from which the trouble started.

Young Jude, eight years old, came to school one morning acting strangely, to say the least. His walk was more than a swagger; it was a decidedly uncertain wobble. Miss Jones had him sit down outside, and later she questioned him. As she listened, only her eyes, usually quiet but now burning with a certain intentness which might be akin to righteous indignation, betrayed her real feelings. After school that day, she went to Ma Kirk's. She entered by the back way, and as was the custom of the community, walked in without knocking, even forgetting to call out as she usually did when entering a house. As she walked through the middle hall she heard voices, and slacked her pace a little. Before she reached the door, she had heard enough to convince her that she had found the selling agent for the Wilkins bootleg crowd. She did not turn back, but reaching the inner door, went into the room where Ma Kirk and Bliney Wilkins were talking. They rose from their seats and stared at Miss Jones when she entered.

"Wal, what ya doin' here?" asked Bliney.

"I want to see you both. I'm glad I happened to find you together." And she proceeded to tell them the story of little Jude and what she thought of a practice that ruined the lives of boys as well as of men and women. Before she had finished, they had listened to a whole sermon on the subject of temperance. Then Miss Jones continued on her way, saying nothing to anyone about what she had heard.

A few days later, the revenue officers cleaned out the Wilkins still and arrested its operators. Where they got their clues, Miss Jones did not know. It was a surprise to her, but no one on earth could convince the mountain people that the teacher had not told. The story spread like wildfire. From that day on, former friends were strangers to her. Some folks crossed the road to avoid meeting her, and one morning a note in scribbled hand containing the following threat was lying on her desk when she came to school: "Miz Jones: You all better to mind yer own bizness if you no wats good fer ya and we mean wat we says."

And now the mayor had asked her to carry an automatic! Well, maybe she should, but she had no desire to do so. Going back into the schoolhouse, she knelt by the desk and asked the Lord to guide her. As she arose, she opened her Bible, and her eyes fell on the opening words of Psalm 121, "I will lift up mine eyes unto the hills, from whence cometh my help. My help cometh from the Lord, which made heaven and earth. He will not suffer thy foot to be moved. . . . Behold, He that keepeth Israel shall neither slumber nor sleep. The Lord is thy keeper. . . . The Lord shall preserve thee from all evil. . . . The Lord shall preserve thy going out and thy coming in from this time forth, and even forevermore."

Then Monty stood in the doorway, waiting for her to go. Down by the river, he tried to show Miss Jones the art of pistol shooting. Several times she tried to hit the floating piece which Monty had thrown into the river. Then she tried other more stationary targets. Once she took aim and fired, and a sycamore ball on a tree across the stream flew to pieces.

"Great," shouted Monty. "That's great, Miss Jones."

"What's great?"

"The way you hit that sycamore ball yonder."

"I wasn't aiming at the sycamore ball. I was aiming at the stick in the river."

"Wal, now—er—Miss Jones!"

"You see, Monty, there's no use. Let's go back to see the mayor."

"Mr. Davey," Miss Jones said to the mayor, "I can't do it!"

"Do what?"

"Carry that pistol around with me. Even if I could hit a target, I wouldn't have any confidence in it. I don't believe it is the thing for me to do. I believe that God will protect me from those who would do me harm."

"Well, you have more faith than I have. I tell you, I don't like to see you go out like that, alone and everything."

"I appreciate your concern, Mr. Davey, and, believe me, I will not unnecessarily place myself in a dangerous position. But I have confidence that if I am placed in such a position, the Lord will care for me."

"All right then, Miss Jones. You go ahead. And remember, when you need help that we can give, let us know."

Several days later, about the middle of the afternoon, Lindy Lee rushed into the schoolroom.

"Miss Jones, Ole Mander Kellan am right nigh to the point of death. She ain't pert nohow. She done told me to get you to come as soon as you could make it. She shore need yore hep. Could you make it this ev'nin'?"

"I'll go after school. Be back here at four o'clock. We'll leave then, and we may be able to get back before dark," replied the teacher.

Four o'clock found Lindy Lee and Miss Jones starting on the ten-mile hike through the woods to Kellan's place. In some places there was a fairly good road to follow, in other places there was a mere footpath about twenty inches wide, girded on both sides by thick shrubs.

It was early fall, and the hike was not without its pleasures. Miss Jones called Lindy Lee's attention to the coloring of the different trees, and, from the beauties of nature about them, tried to draw the girl's thoughts toward God.

Suddenly Lindy Lee, who was in the lead, stopped.

"Miz Jones, there be a man alyin' crost the path."

Sure enough, there was a man lying, face down, right in their way.

"He's probably drunk. You'll have to step over him, Lindy Lee. He won't hurt you," assured Miss Jones.

And Lindy Lee jumped over the man's body. As Miss Jones stepped toward him, preparing to do the same, the man opened his eyes, raised himself on one shoulder, and looked dazedly about.

"What's the trouble, man? Are you sick?" inquired Miss Jones.

"Yas'm, I'm about to be took with one o' them spells I git."

At that, Miss Jones stepped up more closely, felt his pulse, noted his respiration, and looked into his eyes.

"Where do you live?" she asked.

"Down yonder, turn to right about mile and half up the first holler, first house," the sick man answered.

"If you leaned on Lindy Lee and me, could you make it?" and Miss Jones, with Lindy Lee helping, tried to assist the man to his feet. It was evident that he would not be able to stand at all.

They laid him down again, scraped leaves together for a pillow, and made him as comfortable as possible.

"Listen, man. We're going to your house as quickly as we can. We'll get you help. They'll come in a little while and carry you home. I'm sorry we can't carry you."

"Thank ye, Miz Jones," the man said weakly. "I know, now, who ye be."

So Lindy Lee and Miss Jones hurriedly followed the directions given, traveling up the mountain hollow, until at last they found the house.

"Yer man's ailin', down Rattlesnake Path," yelled Lindy Lee.

As they came to the door, Miss Jones explained to the wife the meaning of this abrupt proclamation, and finally guided several boys

from about the place to the sick man. They made a hammock of several blankets and carried him to his home.

When the man had been made comfortable, and everything that could be done under the circumstances had been done, Miss Jones and Lindy Lee started again on their way.

All this had taken time, and even as they neared old Ma Kellan's, the sun was dropping behind the hills.

Coming to a turn in the path, they found a cabin in a small clearing.

Lindy Lee whispered, "This be Tarky's place. I hear tell they make moonshine here."

The place looked deserted, however. There seemed to be no signs of life.

And Miss Jones said, "They must have moved; there seems to be no one here."

"Ye never kin tell," philosophized Lindy Lee, wiser than she knew. For a pair of eyes had seen Miss Jones and the girl coming into sight, and they watched every movement the two made until the woodland hid them from view, on the other side of the cabin.

Things were as Lindy Lee had said. Old Manda was very sick. She had fallen and broken her hip. Doctors from the village seldom bothered to visit the people away back in the hills; so the bones had not been set. She was in great pain, and it was evident that there was no chance for recovery.

When Miss Jones had made her as comfortable as possible, read to her some favorite passages from the Good Book, and prayed with her, it was quite late. Darkness had settled thickly in the valleys and hollows. There was not a ray of light even on the mountaintops.

Praying that the Lord would guide and protect in the homeward walk, she called Lindy Lee and started back.

She turned the switch on her flashlight and lighted the way through the trees. They walked for a mile or so. The moon had not yet risen. Everything was in inky blackness.

"It shore am dark," commented Lindy Lee. "I'm glad you all brought yer flashlight. It brightens things up right smart."

And then the flashlight went out! Readjusting of batteries and bulb failed to bring results. Miss Jones felt in her inner pockets for the extra bulb she usually carried, and then remembered that the one in the flashlight was the extra. She had failed to buy another when the first burned out.

"Lindy Lee, how far is it to the place you called Tarky's?"

"I'd say about two mile. But ye ain't thinkin' of askin' them for help? I'm thinkin' they wish you'd git lost forever out here."

"Lindy Lee, kneel down with me while I pray. It will be hard traveling this path in the darkness, but God can protect us from all the dangers that can possibly come." Even then she would not name the fear that pulled at her heart, but needless to say, it was not the fear of falling in the darkness.

They arose. Miss Jones tucked the useless flashlight away in a pocket. The dim night sky was lighter than the surrounding trees, and by marking the line of light made by the division of the trees above the path, it was possible to discern the general direction and keep in the right way.

To keep cheerful they talked and sometimes sang. Finally, conversation and song lapsed into silence. Guided by the thin line of light, Miss Jones meditated on the lesson portrayed. When she took her eyes from that light, she became confused and fell to one side or the other of the path. By looking again, she could regain the right path, and only by constant upward gaze could she keep it. *How like the Christian way,* she thought as she remembered a poem she had once read. She was starting to tell Lindy Lee about it, when suddenly a powerful flashlight shone out before them, and a voice gruffly called out of the darkness, "What's the idear, Miz Jones? Think ya could git away with this spyin', didn't cha? Wal, ya got another think comin'. Ya'll get no chance to go back and tell the revenuer 'bout this one." And he emphasized his remarks with profanity. Other voices joined his. There was a barking of dogs, and several ran menacingly forward, surrounding Miss Jones. Lindy Lee had dropped to the ground in an attitude of dejection and misery and was crying woefully.

"You stop yer yelpin', Lindy Lee; we ain't wantin' ya. If ya keep quiet, ya'll be all right, ya understand?"

"Yes, sah," meekly whimpered Lindy Lee.

"Whatcha got to say, Miss Jones?"

By this time several lights were shining. She recognized several of the men, the worst characters in the valley. She saw also that there were guns.

"I am not spying. I have been to visit Old Manda. She is very sick. Believe me, I have not come to spy you out."

"How come you didn't have no light then?" put in one.

"Pretty good story, I sez," added another.

"My flashlight burned out," explained Miss Jones. "See, here it is," and she handed it over.

They tried it. Sure enough it was burned out.

She opened her short jacket and held it out on both sides.

"If I were spying on you, I would not come unarmed. But see, I have no pistol."

"What's that abumpin' on the side of your hip?" asked one.

"This is my first-aid kit," and she extended it toward them. "I fastened it on the belt of my skirt."

They came up closer. She felt and smelled their hot liquor-laden breaths and drew back.

"Afraid, be ye? Wal, now, what do ya think of that? Men, this little gal's afraid. Ye better be, sez I." And he moved closer.

"I am not afraid. All my stay in this valley I have tried to do what is right. Today I came not to spy you out, but to help Old Manda, who, as you know, is sick. I would not have been so late on the way, but a man was sick, and we would not leave him."

"That's right, men," a voice broke in. "John Ikes was about to be seized with his fits and she did come and take him on to his house. Telfie, his wife, told me about it."

"Well, that's not sayin' nuthin'. She still coulda been spyin'."

"Well, what ya goin' to do?" impatiently inquired another.

"Here ya been waitin' fer a chance like this all year, and now you act like scairt women. I sez, let's go ahead with the plan."

"Me, too," agreed others.

There was a movement as though they would rush toward her. A few guns were raised.

Instead of retreating, Miss Jones took a step toward them, raised her arms in a gesture calling for silence, and said:

"My friends, you think I am afraid, and I am, but not for myself. I am afraid for you. The God whose will I am trying to carry out, has not only promised that whosoever shall gather against me 'shall fall,' and that no weapon that is formed against me 'shall prosper,' but also that my enemies shall fall before me.

"I am not afraid of death, but I am afraid for those who dare harm me. For you would die in the second death. The plagues would fall upon you, and in the end, fire would come down from heaven and destroy you. Why don't you stop your evil ways; give them up and do right? Jesus will forgive you for your wrongs. Then when He comes, you will be safely ready for Him."

She stopped. There was silent expectancy.

Finally the leader spoke. "Maybe yer right, Miz Jones, maybe yer right. Let her go this time, men. I git to thinkin', and it sorta bothers me. Maybe she's right."

Turning to the teacher, he continued, "Miz Jones, you take yerself off here and go straight down yonder path. Don't look to any way.

There'll be a man followin' ye. It's a shorter way than the way ya come. But ye don't need to note whar it comes out, to take it again. Jis forgit it."

Some men opened the shrubbery on one side of the road, and as a light shone, a small path was revealed.

Miss Jones stepped to the path. Lindy Lee followed closely, and the two walked on. The light from the flashlight of a man behind them lighted the way.

Nothing was said. After what seemed hours, the path opened onto a familiar road.

"Guess you all kin find yer way, now"— and the man turned and left them. When the sound of his footsteps could no longer be heard, Lindy Lee grabbed the teacher's arm and said, "Oh, my soul, Miz Jones, I thought you would be kilt sure by now." And then she thoughtfully added, "If you'da had a pistol, you would hev been, sure enough."

"I guess you're right, Lindy Lee. I guess I would have been killed sure enough." And the teacher lifted her heart in grateful thanks to the greatest Protector. ❧

*S*he'd resisted her conviction that she should go to Fern's bed long enough. Typhoid was raging through the dormitory, and she'd been warned, sternly warned, not to go.
     She went anyway.

I wonder how often we professed Christians devalue the power of intercessory prayer on someone else's behalf. How often we mistakenly assume that generalities work with God. Scripture confirms the truth of this story: only specific prayers work with God.

THE SHADOW

Jean Wingate

*C*ould it be—could it? A moment I stood aghast, then under the impetus of a wild desire, I bounded after the retreating figures of the preceptress and the nurse.

"Mrs. Green," I gasped, in the throes of trying to appear calm. "Really, you should not stay up all night. You can't stand the strain. Let me stay with Fern tonight. Do!" I pleaded.

"Thank you very much, June, for your offer, but I think that Fern's condition is so very serious that special care must be given her tonight. If I find that I need help, I will send for you." And with that the preceptress walked away. How even and cool her words sounded!

Not only Fern, but twenty or more others also were victims of that scourge—typhoid fever. Both dormitories had their long list of patients in various stages of the disease. Some had come very near the gulf, but until the present the deep waters had not passed over.

As in a daze I prepared for the Sabbath. Was there not some way I could manage to be with Fern? My responsibility seemed great, for had I not helped to persuade Fern to come to college this year? I must be with her, that was all there was to it! But how? Plan after plan suggested itself to me, only to be discarded as impossible.

Just what I thought I could do, I didn't know, only—that I *must* see Fern tonight.

Vespers service was especially impressive that evening. As the leader spoke words of faith in God's power to heal, a calmness settled over my turbulent mind, and a conviction came that God still hovered above His own.

It was late that night before I was permitted to think very much of Fern again. Grace and Hope had contracted severe colds. That meant lowered vitality, and was not the Shadow lurking at every door? For about three hours I worked, giving them hot packs, with now and then a glass of steaming lemonade. At last, I greased them well with Vic's salve, bundled them up in chest compresses, and tucked them in bed.

It was now about eleven o'clock. Restlessly I walked the floor.

"June, go to bed," Hope's sleepy voice called out, "or you'll be sick."

"All right, in a minute," I replied. But in a minute she was fast asleep, and I was still pacing the floor.

Desire, in all its human intensity, gripped me. I must go to Fern—I must! Then in saner moments the thought came: *What could I do if I did go? Did I not realize it was against the rule to go upstairs to the sick ward? Had not warnings been given in chapel that very day?*

Finally I could stand it no longer—the human in me gave way. Let the consequences be what they may—go, I must!

I slipped out of my room and made my way down the silent, dimly lighted hall. How the stairs creaked! Something choked me. Would they make a public example of my act? Visions of disgrace danced before me.

· There was the door! I listened. Yes, there was Mrs. Green's voice. But there was also another voice. Probably one of the nurses, I decided.

In a quandary I stood hesitating. Now that I was here, what should I do? Several times discretion got the upper hand, and I started to slip away, but each time a faint moan from within stopped me.

Abruptly the door opened, and one of the nurses peered out.

"Why, June, what are you doing here?" she exclaimed in an audible whisper. "We have been needing someone so much. If—"

"Is that you, June?" broke in Mrs. Green's soft voice. "Why didn't you let us know you were here?" At these words my anxiety fell away as Christian's bundle of old [*Pilgrim's Progress*].

I stepped quickly through the open door, and asked in as businesslike a tone as possible, "Is there something I can do, Mrs. Green?" I heard no reply. I was gazing at the still, grayish-white face. One intent moment I stood there as the truth burned itself into me, then turning, I gasped with an agony I could not hide, "She's dying, Mrs. Green, *she's dying!*"

"I know it," Mrs. Green's even voice replied. Her thin lips drew together in a tighter line, and her fingers twitched nervously, as she bent over the sick girl.

"But what are you going to do?" I demanded impetuously.

"There isn't anything we can do," she returned with the finality of a doctor.

"Have—have you prayed for her?" I ventured.

"Yes," she answered, nodding her head. "We've had prayer for her."

"Special prayer for her alone?" I pressed desperately.

"No, not for her alone, but for all the girls." Mrs. Green stepped to the side of Fern's bed.

"She'll die before morning," I whispered. "Something must be done! Let me go get—some one!"

Mrs. Green hesitated.

"She'll die unless God heals her tonight," I pleaded.

"All right, go."

I dared not wait a second, and before Mrs. Green had time to move or speak, I was gone.

"Grace, Grace," I called out hysterically as I burst through our door, "wake up! Fern is dying, and I'm going after Elder Burke and Elder Mitchel."

Grace, startled at being wakened so suddenly, sat bolt upright in bed. Fern was Grace's roommate.

"O June, you don't say! It surely can't be." Wide-eyed, she stared at me a moment, then flinging the cover off, she exclaimed, "I'm going with you. I'm not going to let you go alone!"

"No, you must not," I remonstrated, kicking off my bedroom slippers, "for you'll get a worse cold and die!" But she paid no heed, and almost before I was ready, she was. Grace grabbed up a worn-out flashlight.

"Perhaps it will do a little good," she whispered as we sped down the corridor to the front door.

How cold and dark it was! Not even the skyline of the hills across the valley was visible. The wind snatched and barked at us as we ran half stumbling down the rocky road to Professor Smith's.

"Professor Smith, Professor Smith!" I called out as we dashed up on his front porch.

"Yes, June, what is it?" came his quick reply. But his name was all I could say. My thoughts refused to express themselves.

"Fern is very sick, Professor Smith," Grace spoke up breathlessly, "and Mrs. Green—"

"She's dying, Professor Smith," I broke in, recovering my voice. "She's dying! Won't you come up immediately? Shall I go for Elder Burke?"

"Yes, go, and I'll be up right away."

Grace and I left the little cottage far behind in a few moments as down the hill and across the railroad tracks to Elder Burke's we ran. Our flashlight kept up a marvelously steady gleam.

Only a minute or two we spent there, then back up the hill, past the girls' dormitory and the other buildings to reach at last the Mitchel home. Our mission there was soon over.

The journey back was considerably slower, for our strength had about given out.

In our room at last, I persuaded Grace (who protested with every breath) to go back to bed. My coat landed in a heap on a chair as I dashed out of the room.

Elder Burke was already there, and in a moment or two Professor Smith arrived, bringing with him Professor Anderson, the vespers speaker of the evening. After a few minutes of silent waiting, Elder Mitchel appeared. They passed quietly in, and the door was shut. Divinity seemed overshadowing us. I sat down on the cot outside and waited, praying with those who prayed inside.

After what seemed but a brief time the door opened and the men filed out. I searched their faces for the answer, but could not tell from their expressions whether God had answered their prayers or not. Despair tried to force itself upon me.

"June, come here!" It was Mrs. Green's voice. Something in her tone, though subdued, electrified me. I was by her side in an instant. Bending, she pointed to Fern's forehead.

"Do you see the perspiration breaking out on her forehead, June? Do you see that faint color spreading over her face?"

Thrilled through every fiber of my being, I cried out, "O Mrs. Green, she will live, she will live! God has healed her!"

And together we wept. 🌿

*L*eprosy is still with us, as you'll discover in this account of Nondis of Papua New Guinea.

What possible hope could there be for a leper?

Miracles. Often we mistakenly assume that they happened only in long-ago times. Not today when we know everything and are capable of everything. For how could a deadly disease such as leprosy possibly be reversible?

NONDIS THE LEPER

Marjorie Lewis Lloyd

The experience of Nondis, a boy of New Guinea, is an incredible one: when a messenger burst into the village of Papua with word that the government patrol was approaching, the people fled in terror. They had never seen white men before, and they were taking no chances. Mothers scooped up their babies; and everybody, young and old, disappeared into the bush or up the mountain. Everybody, that is, except Nondis. He couldn't go, because he was crippled with leprosy!

So when the patrol officers trudged wearily into the village, they found houses empty, cooking fires still burning, and Nondis. Imagine, if you can, his absolute terror as a strange white man in a big hat bent over him and examined him.

Within a week the boy, who knew nothing of the rest of the world, was put aboard a strange aircraft and taken to a leprosarium on the coast. There he was operated upon and sealed in plaster from the soles of his feet to the top of his hips. Think of the trauma of it. No friends. No one could understand his language. He sat alone on his bed day after day, unable even to feed himself because his arms were so deformed.

It was in this condition that a Christian pastor found him and became his friend. He brought him food and clothing, and slowly Nondis learned to speak pidgin. Now the pastor could tell him about Jesus and how He restored the paralytics and healed the lepers. He told him that Jesus is the same today. And the boy believed!

Three months after the plaster was applied, it was cut away. But his joints were still weak and twisted. His left leg was badly ulcerated. It was a terrible disappointment. Now he must be encased in plaster again, this time for six months. But the pastor encouraged him to keep trusting. He told him Jesus still could heal him. And Nondis believed it was true and kept on praying.

On the second Monday night after Nondis was sealed in plaster the second time, he had a dream. In his dream a tall Man in shining white stood by his bed and said to him, "Nondis, it's time for you to get out of bed."

He said, "I can't. Look at me!"

But the Man said kindly. "You *can*! Give Me your hand."

Nondis held out his wasted hand. But the Man said, "No! Open your fingers like this."

"It's not possible. You see, my motor nerves have died, and my hand is permanently disfigured." That's what he had heard the doctors say.

"If you take My hand, your own will straighten." And, in the dream, it was so.

Then the Man in white said kindly, "Now come, get out of bed."

So in his dream Nondis swung his legs over the side of his hospital bed and stood up.

"Go for a walk." And he strode off down the ward.

When he came back to his bed, the Man in the dream said to him, "You have been sick a long time since you first believed, yet your belief in Me hasn't wavered at all. Tonight I have taken away your leprosy and have restored your movement. Now I want you to work for Me."

Nondis said he would, and thanked the Man profusely as He turned and left the room.

Not long after that the boy was awakened by the sound of a patient down the ward calling out. A nurse turned on the light. It was almost dawn anyway, and Nondis decided to say his morning prayer. But in the midst of his prayer he remembered his dream.

Nondis opened his eyes and could hardly believe what he saw. His fingers were straight. He opened both hands several times. It was easy. He examined his formerly twisted arms. He could move them!

Next he felt for his legs. He was happily shocked to discover that the plaster had all crumbled away. The sores had healed, and his joints were strong and firm. Overjoyed, he slipped out of bed and fell to his knees. How could he thank his Lord enough?

When a male nurse passed by, Nondis called him and showed him his hands and his legs. The nurse was astounded at the sight of Nondis standing. The nurse called the other patients to come and see. Excitedly they crowded around him. But some said he shouldn't have removed the plaster. When the doctor came, he cleared that up, however, telling them it was utterly impossible for Nondis to remove the plaster when he couldn't even feed himself.

The doctor examined the boy and said, "I think your God has had something to do with this."

X-rays of his legs were proof of his remarkable healing. Blood tests were negative. Nondis was cleared to return home. But he said to his doctor, "The Lord said I should work for Him, but I really don't know what kind of work I should do. Can you give me some work?"

So Nondis was put to work in the physiotherapy department. That was the beginning. Soon he was transferred to a Seventh-day Adventist hospital, was baptized, and married a lovely Christian girl named Rebecca.

Yes, angels are often sent on missions of healing. But sometimes the Healer is so moved with compassion that He takes charge Himself! ❧

Another Chance

Dawn Boylan

Some miracles are beautiful. Some are not.
This one is very much not—except for the ending.

The shrill ring of the telephone shattered the night. No calls after 10:00 P.M. in the school dormitory, so I knew something must be wrong. Standing at my door, I looked up and down the hall. No one. So I decided to go back to bed. I made my way through the darkness and settled down again. Just then my door flung open, and Mrs. Trenton, the dean, walked in.

"Are you awake?" she asked. "Kari just took two hundred aspirin. We need to get her to the hospital."

Throwing on some clothes, I thought of what had happened that evening. Kari had been really depressed. I knew I should have gone and talked to her, but I had felt so tired.

Guilt gnawed at my conscience now, and I decided to do anything in my power to keep her alive.

I ran with the dean to Betty's house next to the dorm. I wasn't ready for the scene that hit me. Sitting close to the door, Kari was refusing to drink water to wash down the ipecac syrup.

Knowing it was necessary, Betty persisted.

Finally, Mrs. Trenton and I took over. Mrs. Trenton poured the water down Kari's throat while I held her mouth open.

Next we got Kari into Mrs. Trenton's car. The sick feeling in my stomach increased as I wondered whether we would make it to the hospital in time.

The trip to town was long, and I felt unqualified to say anything, but the silence hurt. So I reached for Kari's hand and began to tell her how much we loved her. She spat back, "I don't care."

My fear turned to anger as I realized how selfish she was to do this. What about her parents? What about her friends? What about the faculty? What about the three of us torn apart by her words? Did we even matter?

At the hospital a nurse met us. I helped the nurse rip Kari's clothes off.

The heart monitors intact, we watched. Kari's pulse was racing at 185, her blood pressure 180 over 110. We knew she was really sick.

After a few minutes the doctor walked in and began talking to Kari. I was shocked as he stated that he thought Kari would die.

Kari cried as the doctor pushed the long, plastic tube down her nose. She begged him not to do this. I hurt just watching. With the water and charcoal he was pumping down the tube, her throwing up was inevitable. So I kept myself busy trying to clean her up.

Mrs. Trenton and Betty had walked out to make phone calls, and I began to feel very alone. *Why?* I wondered. *Why would such a beautiful girl end up in a state like this?* Her beauty was now lost somewhere in the midst of all the towels, tubes, monitors, and vomit.

Just three days ago I had done some fast talking and convinced Kari to stay at our Christian school. But somehow I had gone wrong. Maybe I shouldn't have tried to make her stay. My heart cried out for my mistakes and for this girl lying here dying.

I snapped to the present as Kari started talking to me. "Why don't they just let me die? Can't you understand that my problems are too big for me to handle? Just let me die."

Her frustration was clear, and I could feel what she was feeling. I remembered times when I'd felt as if I couldn't live through another day. But I tried to reassure her.

The nurse returned to the room, and I began to feel more at ease. Then I glanced at the monitor. Instantly Kari's pulse jumped to 250, and I knew we had problems.

Looking up, the nurse asked me if I'd ever responded to a code, when someone goes into cardiac arrest. I told her I had, and I felt my hands get clammy. She went on to tell me, "When it happens, hit the door, yell 'doctor,' and get back in here as fast as you can."

"This is no time for wimps," I told myself. But now I wished I hadn't come. I had watched only one other person die—a stranger—and it had been hard. If Kari died and I saw it, I would feel the effects for a lifetime.

Fight

Inside I whispered a prayer. *God, if she dies, please don't let Mrs. Trenton and Betty see it.* I knew the pain they were having as faculty, and I begged God to spare them any further pain.

Kari's pulse stabilized. Then more bad news came. They couldn't fly Kari to a bigger hospital because of blizzard conditions in both Salt Lake City and Grand Junction. And Moab hospital wasn't equipped for such emergencies.

I looked at the doctor, hoping for reassurance. But he only said, "It's going to be a hard night."

My faith was beginning to waver. Why was this happening? Suddenly it hit me. This wasn't my fault. It wasn't the school's fault. It was sin's fault. Satan caused this. Kari was a sick girl. She had a disease called depression, and Satan was working hard to kill her.

Gradually I worked up the courage to do what needed to be done. I knew Kari wouldn't live unless she wanted to. And I had one more chance to help her.

"Kari," I stammered, "I want to ask you a favor."

She looked away and bitterly asked what.

"I want to ask you to fight tonight. Fight like you've never fought before. Do it for me, Kari. I love you, and I want you to live. Please, Kari."

She was quiet for a minute. "I guess I will," she replied reluctantly.

"Kari, I'm serious about this. This isn't a game. I'm not playing with you. If you promise, do it wholeheartedly."

She said quietly, "I'll fight."

Relief flooded over me. I knew things were in God's hands now. Mrs. Trenton, Betty, and I followed as the nurse wheeled Kari's bed down to the intensive care unit. We tried once more to clean her up; then, deciding there was no more we could do, we got ready to leave.

I watched as the dean said goodbye. I wondered what I would say when it was my turn. Walking up to Kari, I felt her grab me and pull me close. Her kiss was mingled with tears. A kiss of anguish, of despair, of hopelessness.

Walking down the hall, I felt utterly dirty. Vomit covered me. I thought about how none of us is exempt from sin. All of us are sinners who desperately need Christ.

I wiped vomit off my face and felt a tear make a trail down my cheek.

Prayer

On the way back to the school, I listened to Mrs. Trenton sorting out her feelings. As we pulled onto campus, we decided to go to the principal's home for some support. We had drained ourselves, and we needed to recuperate.

Mr. Tilman opened the door very groggy-eyed, and soon Mrs. Tilman came into the living room too. We discussed what had happened and decided to pray. Kneeling down, I felt a twinge of bitterness. The prayer dragged on, and although my prayer was sincere, I felt resentment.

Why are we praying? I thought. *The worst is over.*

After the prayer, we went back to the girls' dorm and I cleaned up. Then I tried to get some sleep, but by the time I drifted off, I had only one hour before I needed to be at work.

I got up feeling grouchy. I was upset over my own incapacity to know the right things to say and do. And I began to question God again. Why had He even let this happen?

After breakfast I found myself shrugging off the problem. But all the feelings crashed down on me when I reached the dorm again. There I learned the rest of the drama. At 3:30 A.M., the very time Mrs. Trenton, Betty, and I were on our knees with the Tilmans, Kari's heart had started fibrillating and had gone completely off the heart monitor.

But by some miracle, Kari's heart started beating again, and she regained consciousness. At the very time I had been doubting our need of God, the very time I was resenting prayer, God had worked a miracle. He had saved Kari's life.

This hit me full in the face. Even for a selfish, depressed high school senior, God had worked a miracle. And He worked a miracle for me too, despite my bitterness. He gave both Kari and me another chance. ❧

*O*h, it is so dark—so dark," she breathed. "How can I ever hurry?"

Then she lost her path again.

And again . . .

Today, we are so blinded by ever-present light that it may be hard for us to conceptualize what it must have been like a century ago. Or, even today, in much of the unindustrialized world. Is it possible God steps in so rarely in our lives today because our actions tell Him we feel technology enables us to get along without Him just fine?

THE LIGHTED PATH

Mrs. R. B. Sheffer

Mary Parsons wakened suddenly, startled by an insistent rapping at the door of the cottage; or was she only dreaming? No, she was wide awake now, her hand groping about on the night stand for the matches. The rapping continued, followed by a familiar voice as the gleam from the hastily lighted kerosene lamp penetrated the darkness.

"Don't be frightened, Mary; it is just I, your neighbor Bob Steadman. Nan is sick, and she wants you to come as quickly as you can. I hated calling you, knowing that Jim is away and you are alone here with the children."

"That's all right, Bob," Mary reassured him. "They are all sound asleep and will be safe and snug here. I'll be ready in just a few moments." Already she was dressing swiftly.

"Thank you, Mary," answered the voice at the door; "I'll run along now. I promised Nan I'd be right back. You know how she dreads being alone, especially when she gets one of her nervous spells."

Yes, Mary Parsons *did* know, for she had helped Bob bring Nan through more than one of those nervous heart attacks, to which his wife was subject, and middle-aged Nan Steadman had grown accustomed to depending on her calm, poised, efficient young neighbor whenever she felt one of her nervous spells coming on.

Mary, fully dressed now and carrying her lighted lamp, looked into the next room at three sleeping children. She noted by the clock that it was not yet midnight. What if baby sister in her crib should waken, as she sometimes did in the middle of the night? What if the two little boys should be roused and, finding their mother gone, become frightened? So, tiptoeing over to the cot where small Leslie, the eldest of the three, lay peacefully sleeping, she shook him gently. "Leslie," she whispered softly as he opened sleepy eyes, "Auntie Steadman is sick and Mother must go for a little while to help her. You will be all right, but if Van or baby sister should waken, just be sure they are covered against the chill air, and remember, Jesus will take care of you. Mother will not be gone long. Do you hear me, Leslie?"

The eyelids fluttered open again for an instant; there was the faintest nod, and then as his mother turned the light low and placed the lamp on a high shelf where it shone faintly into the children's room. She was relieved to see that already Leslie was sleeping soundly again, but she trusted that should he be wakened he would remember her words and would not be frightened by her absence.

She slipped on a light coat and wrapped a scarf about her head and throat, for although it was late summer, the nights held a sharp chill.

Once outside, she'd had taken only a few steps before she realized how very dark a moonless night could be. A haze had spread over the sky, obscuring even the stars; and between the Parsons' home and that of their nearest neighbors, the Steadmans, was a narrow, winding trail which led down through a draw, up over a sandy knoll, then for a short distance it ran parallel with a barbed-wire fence, then under the fence and into a patch of wild-plum bushes, where the zigzag path was bordered on either side by the sharp-thorned, shoulder-high bushes which grew in great profusion in the Steadmans' pasture lot. Mary started to turn back for the lantern, but then she remembered that Jim, her husband, had taken it with him that week on his trip with the neighborhood threshing crew over into the next township. There was nothing to do but to go on, hoping that her eyes would become accustomed to the darkness, and that she would be able to keep to the trail.

It was not hard to find her way down past the well and through the draw; nor was it too difficult to keep to the path up over the grassy knoll; for here the sandy trail was in sharp contrast to the crisp, dry grass on either side. But soon she was leaving the path, and now there should be the corner post of the fence. Yes, here it was. Her fingers felt along up the guy wire, over the top of the post to the top wire; then by letting her fingers travel very lightly and cautiously along the barbed wire, she was able to follow the fence through the soft plowed ground. She counted the posts to the place where she must stoop and crawl under.

Yes, there was the path. She could feel the footprints. But now she must follow the narrow, winding path which wound around between the plum bushes growing on all sides, up almost to the Steadmans' dooryard.

Mary was trying to hurry, as she knew the need of bringing speedy relief to her sick friend, and she could easily imagine what a difficult time Bob must be having with his near-hysterical wife.

Contrary to her expectations of becoming accustomed to the darkness, it seemed to have grown only more dense. She was forced several times to stoop down and feel about in the soft sandy soil for the footprints to guide her back to the path.

"Oh, it is so dark—*so dark,*" she breathed. "How can I ever hurry?" Had she lost the path? Yes. No, there it was again, the print of Bob's heavy boots in the soft earth. *Now* she would hurry; surely she knew every twist and turn of the narrow path from here on! But soon she was brought to a halt sharply by running up against a wire fence. She must find her way, again, back to the trail. Ah! Here it was again; she felt with her fingers for the footprints. The path was wider here; *she would hurry now*!

But fear of losing her way made her progress slow. "Oh," she breathed again, "if only I had a little light! Just a *little light*." Mary was fairly panting from her efforts to hurry in the intense darkness, her fear of becoming lost in the thicket, and her anxiety for her sick neighbor.

Then suddenly there it was right in front of her—a little square patch of light, somewhat larger than her footprints. Startled, she stopped short. Where did the light come from? Mary looked up over her shoulder, but only darkness met her gaze. She stepped forward into the patch of light; as she did so it advanced. She quickened her pace and there, step by step, as she moved swiftly along the path, was the light just ahead of her, guiding her safely, surely, till she reached the Steadmans' dooryard. Then the light disappeared, and there in front of her was the light from the kitchen window. There was only time for a hurried "Thank You, Lord," and Mary Parsons ran swiftly the intervening steps to the doorway, where she was met by the anxious husband of her sick friend.

"Nan's terrible bad, Mary; I'm so glad you are here," he said in a relieved tone. "No one else can do for Nan what you can. You sure made good time!"

"Did I?" gasped Mary. "I thought I'd never get here! It seemed hours, until the light came!"

There was no time to explain. Mary hurried to the bedside of the sufferer. Bob's helplessness vanished under young Mary's deft leadership, and he helped her give the soothing treatments which always seemed to work like magic in relieving the tense nerves of the distraught woman.

It was several hours later, in the very darkest hours of the night, just before the dawn, that finally Mary could leave her neighbor's side. She was so utterly weary that the earlier experience of the night never once entered her mind as she stepped out into the darkness from the dimly lighted room where already Nan Steadman was sleeping peacefully, and Bob was lying down on a nearby couch for a much-needed rest. She might have asked for the lantern had she remembered; but it was not until she was at the very edge of the plum thicket that Mary sensed her need. She was wondering whether she should retrace her steps and secure the lantern, when once again that magic square of light appeared just a little to one side and directly in the middle of the sandy trail, guiding her back to the path. Again Mary Parsons looked up over her shoulder and about her in every direction; but there was no light anywhere except that mysterious square there on the path.

Thankfully, she took that one step and then the light moved on ahead; and so forgetting her weariness she sped swiftly, surely home to the children. There was no anxiety now, only a deep sense of relief and a great joy in her heart. For surely the One who sent that light to guide her footsteps had also been watching over her little ones at home alone. Not until she was once again in her own dooryard did the light disappear. Breathing a prayer of thankfulness, she unlocked the door and tiptoed her way into the nursery, where she found the three children still fast asleep.

Just for a moment ere she crept back into

her own bed for a little rest before the dawn should come, with its many duties, Mary knelt by her bedside.

"Thank You, dear Lord, for sending the light," she whispered gratefully.

Then, as she laid her head on the pillow, she tucked one more precious experience (like a priceless gem, for safekeeping) into her box of treasured memories, never to be forgotten so long as life should last. ❧

SECTION FIVE

"I will answer them before they even call to me. While they are still talking to me about their needs, I will go ahead and answer their prayers!"
Isaiah 65:24 (NLT)

*M*rs. Garrett sat bolt upright in bed, having heard a voice in the darkness. But, after her husband went back to sleep, she wasn't so sure. But then she heard it again!

Society in general makes a big deal of extrasensory perception. However, I submit that such a phenomenon divorced from a personal relationship with God oftentimes leaves one incapable of doing anything to prevent catastrophe from happening. But with God—that is an entirely different matter.

HE SHALL GIVE HIS ANGELS CHARGE

Leta Walker

*P*enny is in danger!"

Mrs. Garrett sat upright in bed and stared into the darkness. Not a thing could she see; not a sound could she hear except the heavy breathing of her husband. But certainly someone had spoken!

"Will! Will!" she whispered, shaking the sleeping man by the shoulder. "Will, wake up! Something is wrong with Penny." Now it was Mr. Garrett's turn to be frightened.

"Where is she?" and he swung his feet over the side of the bed to the floor.

"I don't know. She went for a ride early this evening with Larry. But there's something wrong; *I know there is*!"

Mr. Garrett heaved a sigh of relief as he lay down again. "Oh, you're just nervous; she'll be all right." And he promptly went back to sleep.

But it was not so easy for Mrs. Garrett to resume her interrupted rest. The words she had heard kept ringing in her ears as she lay with closed eyes, trying to relax.

Just as she was dozing off, again came the warning, *"Penny is in danger."* The disturbed mother began to pray; she prayed for the protection of the girl who at that moment was thinking, *We'll all be killed together.* She prayed until she heard a step on the porch; then, with fear nearly choking her, she rushed to the door.

The headlights of the automobile cut a path of light through the midnight blackness. The car hurtled onto the main pavement from a narrow dirt road, barely missing a huge tanker, and Penny bounced until her head hit the top. Desperately she clutched the seat and gritted her teeth as the car roared down the highway and swerved around sharp curves. One minute it lurched toward the bank, the next toward the cliff. Larry frantically fought the wheel as

Cimmerian darkness rushed toward them. Finally they seemed to hang suspended in air over the cliff, for Penny looked down, down—far down—through the windshield. Then she closed her eyes, every muscle tensed as, with one swift glance into the future, she saw the car lying in a crumpled mass at the foot of the cliff—four lives blotted out. She thought, *We'll all be killed together.* She waited for the car to somersault through space; she waited for the quick stab of pain and blessed unconsciousness. But nothing happened. All was quiet, motionless.

Penny opened her eyes. So sure had she been of death that it took her a moment to realize that she was looking not *down* but *out*.

"Are you hurt?" That was Larry, white-faced, worried, fighting to keep the terror out of his voice. She could not speak; she could only shake her head with a twisted grin that she tried to make nonchalant and reassuring.

In the backseat Margy was sobbing hysterically, and Jim was trying to quiet her. "Either one of you hurt?" Larry asked, not daring to move lest any motion should jar the automobile from its precarious perch. "Just scratched a little," came the reply. "But how are we going to get out of here?"

The car was tipped on its side, and Penny's heart beat a wild tattoo as Larry wormed through his window, then reached in a hand to help her out. It was the only way of exit. But finally all four of the young people were standing in a huddled group on the pavement.

As the boys struggled to right the automobile, over and over to Penny came the thought, *It happened because Larry was angry. And we might all have been killed.* As she walked to the front of the car, she wondered what had kept them on the road. In the soft dirt on the bank were wheel tracks to the very edge of the cliff, but the car had come to a standstill several feet

from the edge. Then she saw what had saved them. The bumper had hooked on a cable stretched between posts along the side of the highway; and as a result the car was swung back onto the pavement, leaving one post uprooted and several loosened. Penny marveled. It was a miracle!

A sobered group drove the rest of the way home. The experience seemed like a bad dream to Penny. She could hardly force her shaking legs to carry her the short distance from the car to the porch.

Her mother met her at the door. "What happened, Penny?"

The girl stared. No one had seen the mishap; no one but the occupants of the car knew about it. How had her mother heard? She tried to sound truthful as she answered, "Why, nothing."

"You had an accident, didn't you?"

"Yes," Penny answered wonderingly. "But how did you know?"

"It was about ten o'clock"—and here Penny's heart skipped a beat, for that was about the time the car had been spinning toward the cliff—"I heard a voice say, 'Penny is in danger.' And I began to pray."

Penny knew then. It had not been the posts or the cable stretched between them; it had not been luck. It had been her mother's prayer that had saved her life. ❧

Ralph wondered that night whether prayer was nothing more than a formality, a mechanical act, a habit that didn't really mean anything. But, then, he felt he ought to pray anyhow. Why, he didn't really know.

Prayer. How often are our prayers merely perfunctory? Something muttered from habit divorced from awareness. But what if we truly believe, as we pray, that God will protect us? With that in mind, let's listen to Louis Pettis as he tells us his story.

DANGER IN THE DARK

Louis W. Pettis

As Ralph walked into the warmth of the kitchen and kicked a bit of dry snow from his shoe, his father looked up with a smile and a question.

"I'm glad you're in early, Ralph," he said. "Now I'll not be wondering about you. I hope you had a good time skating; it's great exercise. By the way, what's the weather like?"

"It's good and cold, Dad," answered his twenty-year-old son. "I wish you didn't have to be going to work at a time when most people can be warm and cozy at home. You ought to be going to bed now, not out to work. It will hit ten below tonight, I think."

"You're right, son, these night jobs are not the best; but work is scarce, and I couldn't pass up this big order of painting in the downtown department store. We have to paint at night while there are no customers or clerks in our way."

"How soon will you be leaving, Dad?"

"I'm going to prepare a lunch and eat first. Probably I'll be here about a half hour yet."

"Do you mind if I go to bed, Dad? My work will be hard tomorrow, and I'd better try to get plenty of sleep."

"Why, no, son," Mr. Corwin answered heartily, "you go right up to bed and get your sleep."

"All right, I'll do it. Good night, Dad. Take care of yourself."

"I will. Good night, Ralph."

A warm smile played over Mr. Corwin's face as he set a pot of water to boil to make himself a drink. To himself he was happily thinking: *He's a good boy—doesn't cause me any trouble, and appreciates what little I can do for him.*

Upstairs Ralph got into his flannel pajamas before studying his Bible. Having finished his study, he lay on his back for a few minutes, staring at the ceiling, before getting on his knees.

Dear old Dad, he was thinking. *I wish he'd give his heart to the Lord. He has many wonderful qualities, but he'll never get anywhere till he gives in and starts living the way he knows he should. Well, I must keep praying for him.*

Ralph slipped down to a kneeling position on the floor beside the bed, and, beginning with his father, named the different persons on his prayer list; for he loved intercessory prayer and was praying for a number of friends and relatives.

When he had finished praying for the names on his list, he was silent before the Lord for a few moments. During this little interval, he thought to himself: *I guess I ought to ask the Lord to take care of me through the night. I've done this every night since I became a Christian at thirteen. But sometimes I wonder if it's really necessary. Nothing ever happens around here at night. Now if I were driving a truck or flying a plane through a night of violent storm—but here I'm perfectly safe . . .*

Still, the habit of his early teen years was too strong to be resisted; he ended his prayer with a simple but fervent request that the protecting care of God would enfold him and all his dear ones during the long hours of darkness.

Ten minutes later he was enwrapped in that deep and unwaking sleep of a healthy, vigorous young man whose weary body called for sound sleep that would be unresponsive to all sounds, sights, and smells.

At 9:45, about ten minutes after Ralph fell asleep, Mr. Corwin put the lid down on the coffeepot, bundled up in his heavy overcoat, picked up his overalls and tools, turned out the kitchen light, and went out into the biting cold of the winter night.

In the house all was dark and quiet—almost. For there was pale-blue light in the kitchen, with the gentle rustle of a boiling liquid. The light came from a gas burner whose flame was turned down low, the sound from the coffeepot, whose contents were simmering away.

But there was no one around to see the soft blue glow or hear the murmuring sound from the coffeepot. Only Ralph was in the house, and he was asleep upstairs.

If someone had been listening, he would have heard, after a few minutes, a new sound. It was gentle, it was distinct, it was different; and its difference would have conveyed meaning to the listener. He would have heard a slight metallic knock, as of a metal lid rising a little and falling softly back on the rim of the container. Under a brighter light an observer, had there been one, could have seen the lid of the coffeepot flutter a bit as it was forced upward; the coffee was boiling harder now.

Ralph slept on.

Now the gentle sound gave way to a hiss, and then a sputter. In a few seconds, this stopped and the pale-blue light went out. Then the only sound was a soft whisper as the gas sighed its way past the lips of the gas jets and escaped into the freedom of the kitchen.

There was no hurry, no violence. Slowly and gently the deadly vapor filled the kitchen, rolled into the dining room, and then silently climbed the stairs and sidled into the room where Ralph lay sleeping. Because of the severe cold outside, he had gone to bed with the windows closed and the hall door open. So there was nothing to bar or to thin down the poisonous cloud that began to gather about Ralph's defenseless unprotected head.

Into his nostrils went the fatal gas, with its power to induce sleep first and death next.

Ralph could do nothing to save himself. He was a sound sleeper under normal conditions, never waking till called in the morning. His father would not be back until after seven o'clock in the morning.

As Ralph's wristwatch and his heartbeats steadily ticked off the moments of life, the percentage of gas in the room rose higher and higher, while the gas jets in the kitchen without hurry and without cessation insistently released their death-bringing fumes into the air.

Ralph's luminous dial showed one o'clock in the morning. For more than three hours, the death cloud had been pushing closer to the sleeping young man.

And then God spoke.

"You'd better wake up, Ralph!"

The deep breathing stopped. Ralph came up from way down under, troubled. *Something's wrong! Who told me to wake up? Was it Dad? Hey! What's that I smell? Why, the room is full of gas!*

Then God spoke again: *"Don't light a match or touch a light switch!"*

And Ralph, coming out of a deep sleep, got the message at once. His mind instantly alert, he knew what to do. First he ran to the one upstairs room with a closed door. There he breathed a few times to clean his lungs and then fill them with untainted air; he knew the gas would be stronger downstairs.

Holding a big lungful of air, his heart pounding madly, he felt his way through the upstairs blackness until his feet found the stairway. Step by step downward he groped, profoundly thankful for his lifelong habit of memorizing the number of steps in any stairs he used frequently. Ah, the downstairs hall floor! Good! Now to the kitchen, with its steady whisper of flowing gas. A few seconds more to find the stove in the black kitchen and turn the handle to shut off the gas. Lungs were bursting as he rushed to the back door, opening it to the star-sprinkled night and standing there to gulp the freshness of the below-zero air into his lungs.

A few moments later, Ralph opened the front door of the house.

"I know it will soon be cold in here," he said aloud, "but I won't mind as long as I get this gas out!"

He went to bed in that upstairs room whose door had been closed; but before turning the covers back, he had a special prayer meeting.

"Dear Lord," he cried, "I thank You for saving my life tonight! I could never have awakened if it hadn't been for You! Oh, I'm so thankful! And I am the one who was thinking that I'm never in danger; I almost didn't ask You to take care of me through this night. But how thankful I am that in my younger days I formed the habit of placing my life in Your hands every night and claiming the promise of protection! Dear Father, help me to never forget this miracle. Help me to always be faithful, and if it please You, help me to be a worker for You someday."

And then, knowing he was perfectly safe in God's hands, Ralph went to sleep. ❧

*T*he fog was so thick that morning that the three teenagers felt they could almost cut it with a knife.

Then ghostly headlights just ahead on their side of the road!

Fourteen years ago, my wife and I experienced something we've never been able to eradicate from our conscious memory: twin headlights racing across the median into our SUV—a dreaded head-on collision we assumed (during the nanosecond interval before the crash) would be fatal. But God wasn't through with us yet. This book would otherwise not have been born.

Angels in the Fog

Lois Foreman

Crash! Thud! Oh, sickening, dreaded sound—the impact of two automobiles smashing together, then bouncing apart and rolling on for a few yards.

How well I remember that awful morning, the first day of October, a few years ago. I had learned to drive the summer before, and that fall my brother Don and another boy, Dean by name, and I began driving to high school, which was twenty-five miles from our home. All had gone well, and I was beginning to gain more confidence in myself, which is one of the needed factors in a good driver's makeup.

This particular morning, when we finally got the sleep rubbed from our eyes, we found the outside world enveloped in one of those fogs that seem to be thick enough to cut with a knife and impenetrable by any light beyond the distance of a few feet. As our family knelt for morning worship, I, as usual, offered a silent prayer that our journey to school and back might be a safe one; however, this trip caused more anxiety in my heart than the first trip alone without an experienced driver had caused.

"Well, I think we'd better get started, Lois, don't you?" asked my brother. It was seven-fifteen—about fifteen minutes earlier than we usually started.

"Yes, perhaps we should, because the visibility is so poor and we'll have to drive slowly," I answered. We gathered up our books and lunches, and went out to the car.

"Drive slowly and don't take any chances. Be just as careful as you can, and I hope you'll run out of this when you get to the other side of Ottawa. Be good and be careful." These were the words of my mother as I started the engine and released the clutch.

"We'll do our best," we assured her as the car rolled down the drive.

Dean was waiting for us as usual, and when we suggested that he sit in the front seat with Don and me, he responded, "Yes, I think I will," a thing which he had never done before.

Everything went well until we came around a curve only five miles from our destination. Suddenly, what should we see before us but a glimmer of two headlights on our side of the road. They continued to come closer, and through the fog we began to see the outline of a small delivery truck which the car on our side of the road was trying to pass. I slackened my speed and applied the brakes in the hope that the other driver would either see us and go back to his side of the road or speed around the truck and into his own lane before we got there. No such thing happened, however. He came right along on our side of the highway. In an effort to avoid a head-on collision, I drove off the road onto the wide shoulder, but it happened to be rough in this particular spot, which made steering hard at the speed we were going, and just as we came even with the back wheel of the other vehicle, a bump threw us over into it. How well I remember seeing that large maroon object bounce off our left front fender as we rolled on for a short distance along the highway. When we came to a stop, we all got out to see just what had been smashed and how badly.

The two men who were the occupants of the truck came running toward us calling, "Anyone hurt?"

"No," we all three replied simultaneously.

They were two of the most friendly men I have ever met under such circumstances. Not only did they advise us to get the name, address, and license number of the other car, but they volunteered to be our witnesses, should we need any to prove that we were in no way to blame for the accident.

By this time, the driver of the other car had estimated the damage he had suffered, and approached our group. We were pleasantly surprised that he didn't seem angry.

"Who was driving?" he asked.

"I was," I answered, trembling.

"You are a very fine driver, little lady," he told me. "I've been thanking my lucky stars that I'm still alive. I can't understand why I didn't see you coming, but I did not notice you at all. I'm so thankful you are such a good driver."

"You'd better give the young people your name and address and license number," one of the men from the truck suggested.

"Yes, of course. My insurance company will make all of this all right," he assured us. "You just have your garage man repair your car and send the bill to me." Then he wrote his name and address and the name and address of his insurance company on a piece of paper, and handed it to me.

After some debate, it was decided that we should not attempt to drive our car on into town, even though it had only a crumpled fender, a sprung wheel, and a rim so bent that the inner tube could be seen. Two boys who attended the same school we did came along about this moment and stopped to see what was going on; so we decided to ride into town with them.

When we went to get our lunches, books, and other belongings from the car, we found them thrown all over the backseat and floor. Dean questioned, "What would have happened to me if I had been back there?"

"Dean, you just weren't supposed to sit back there today," I answered.

That night when school was over, the garage man had our car in good enough shape for us to drive it, but we found that we would have to wait for new parts which had been ordered to make the job complete.

Several days later we heard from the insurance company, filled out several questionnaires, and secured the signatures of the witnesses to the accident. In due time we received payment for the damages.

Whenever we discussed the incident later, the boys always said that the only words spoken at the moment were, "Oh, I hit him," which I cried out just when we crashed. But I know that many other thoughts went through our minds, and I am sure a heavenly angel directed me to drive off the road to the safer shoulder.

Our mother, at home, was praying for our safety. As she worked about the house, she continually thought of us and breathed almost a continuous prayer to the Father above.

In a far-off city my sister, who had been impressed that Don and I were in danger, was also praying. When she heard about the accident, she told the woman with whom she was staying, a friend of the family, about the experience, and the friend said: "I didn't say anything to you that morning, not wishing to alarm you, but I was awakened from a sound sleep about eight-thirty, and it seemed as though a voice said to me, 'Pray for the children: they are in danger.' Immediately I knelt and prayed for their protection and safety."

It happened that eight-thirty was about the time our accident occurred.

I have often thought of the experience and thanked God for His protection. He can and will likewise protect and care for anyone who will trust in His keeping power. ❧

*I*t was in the cold and snowy winter of 1978–1979 that Steve and Roxann Hamilton had to make an emergency trip over the Sierra Nevada.

I envy people such as my cousin Steve Hamilton the phenomenal memory that enables them, even many years after experiencing something, to retell the story in detail exactly as it happened. Had I tried to re-create such an event a third of a century later, so much would have been indistinct. But this is why this account is so riveting: my cousin not only can, but did, for this book.

MIRACLE ON HIGHWAY 88

Steve Hamilton

We left late, so it was nearing eight o'clock at night before we got to the top of Carson Pass on Highway 88.

The temperature was near zero as we passed Caples Lake and wound our way over the summit and started down the other side. Here we encountered the aftermath of a very rare ice storm. The west slope at that point was solid ice. It had turned too cold to snow, but there was about a half inch of very dry fine powder on top of the ice. We could not have even stood or walked on it, much less have driven a one-ton long-bed pickup, even with oversized tires and aggressive tread. I had driven that exact stretch of road dozens and dozens of times in the last several years commuting from Fresno to Carson City, but never had I faced anything like this.

We rounded a gentle curve, and there was a long fairly straight stretch—maybe three-fourths of a mile in length. It was a little steeper. Up to our right was a ridge where in the 1960s there had been a ski slope known as Peddler Hill. The other side of the road was a sheer cliff with an eight-hundred-foot to one-thousand-foot drop. Cal-Trans, which maintained California's highways, had worked all fall blasting rock and making it a little wider and a little safer, but early and continuous storms had prevented them from installing guard rails along the left hand on our downhill sides. Furthermore, the snow and ice buildup of several inches filled in the ditches and the pavement was flush with the side of the road, thus there was nothing to prevent a vehicle from going over the cliff.

We were only moving at about fifteen to eighteen miles per hour, and down at the bottom of the grade we could see emergency lights flashing. I started tapping my brakes. Tapping them is all I could do and still keep control of our truck. Finally, I told Roxann, "We are completely unable to stop or even slow down." I kept tapping them anyway, hoping we would find a little friction somewhere.

It was full moon, and it was almost like daylight. About a thousand feet ahead, we could see why the flashers were flashing. A car coming uphill had slid off the road on the inside bank and was partially down in the ditch and small creek. A tour bus was coming uphill toward us and had partially spun out heading towards the same ditch and culvert where the car was. The rear end of the bus was swung around toward the cliff on the other side of the road. Roxann and I quickly discussed it and felt there was barely enough room to get around the bus, provided we did not hit the bus and ricochet over the cliff.

Though I was still tapping the brakes, we were still going about twenty miles per hour. I lined up the vehicle so we could go around. When we were about three hundred feet away, the driver of the car off in the ditch scrambled around on our side of the bus trying to get the driver to open the passenger door. He slipped on the ice and fell down right in front of us.

He tried to get up but he just kept falling and moving farther out into our lane. I told Roxann that if I tried to go around the bus, we would likely kill the person in the road, so I'd need to go to the inside and try to rub against the bank on her side and slow us down so we could survive the impact. We eased over onto the snowbank, and the snow started flying. Then we hit a metal snow pole and sheared it off. It bounced over our cab and landed in our truck bed. That little impact forced us into the bank too hard, and we started careening toward the cliff. We had several feet of snow on our hood and on top of the cab, so I could hardly see a thing. I couldn't even tell which direction we were going.

Roxann could see out her window, however, and she cried out that we were going over the cliff.

Her next words were, "God, stop us!" *Instantly,* we stopped. Not *gradually*—but *instantly.* I still could not see where we were. Looking out her window, Roxann could only see hundreds and hundreds of feet of space, no bank at all.

As I started to get out, I could feel the truck rock a little. The truck was on a pivot, high-centered right under where we were sitting. We were turned so our right wheel was hanging off the bank. My door still opened over the edge of the road, but I didn't dare get out—the truck might tip.

The man who had fallen in the road made his way over to us and held on to the rear part of the truck. He put some weight on it. While we were debating as to what to do, a Cal-Trans pickup arrived on the scene. It had four-wheel drive, tire chains, and a front mounted winch. There were two men in it—one hopped out and climbed up into the rear part of the bed with one foot on the bumper. Just as the driver was going to attach the winch cable, another pickup came careening down the hill. If he hit us, we were all history. Fortunately, he was a good driver and didn't even brake, just drove his truck into the big snowbank between two large fir trees, just missing the other car in the ditch.

The Cal-Trans pickup driver finished hooking the cable onto us, and since he had chains on, too, we thought he could pull us back into the road. It didn't even budge us! It even winched his truck towards the bank.

The man who had fallen down in front of us grabbed a large light from the Cal-Trans man and found footing right next to the uphill bank and walked briskly uphill trying to get far enough up to stop anymore cars.

The Cal-Trans pickup driver had disconnected and backed up to get a better angle. The bus had been backed down the hill about a hundred feet and had gotten straightened up. Just then here came a flatbed truck down the hill. The driver couldn't stop, and we all thought, *Oh no, not again!* But with the bus moved, he was able to drive through without braking, and thus missed us.

By now the man with the flashlight was up near the top, and he stopped all further cars.

A large Cal-Trans snowplow with chains arrived. It was also a sand truck, and it sprayed sand all over us all wonderfully. Now we could stand up. Roxann *finally* was able to get out. She was permitted to get in the cab of the snowplow.

She was a wonderful mother, and I distinctly remember her saying as she emerged from the cab of our truck, clutching year-old Amee, "Thank You, Lord, for saving my baby." Not thinking about herself, she was praising the Lord for saving her baby!

The snowplow hooked on to us and easily pulled us back on the road. Now, all hands went over and studied the site. Cal-Trans drivers were dumbfounded. There was no bank—no berm or levee. Not even any grease on the ice showing where the truck had rested. They concluded it was a miracle: "There was nothing to have kept you from going over at all."

The Cal-Trans pickup driver walked me back up the road about fifty feet, took his big light and shined it over the cliff and said, "Look down there." The high intensity beam illuminated a red-and-white VW bus wedged between two trees about three or four hundred feet below. "That happened last weekend, and those folk weren't so lucky. Three people died. It took a couple of days to even get the bodies out!"

I told him about Roxann's prayer. All he said was, "Tell ya what, I'm a believer!"

"And it shall come to pass, that before they call, I will answer; and while they are yet speaking, I will hear!" (Isaiah 65:24). ❧

*T*he firefighters' hearts all but failed them, for they were locked in by a four-sided wall of fire. A firefighter's worst nightmare.

Then, suddenly . . .

It is said that, in wartime, "there are no atheists in foxholes." One of the things that amazes me most about God is His absence of pride. Wouldn't you think He'd say, in instances such as this one, "Now, this man who hasn't given Me the time of day since he was a child—now that he's facing certain death unless I step in—well, it's just too late! You should have communicated with Me when you had a chance." But instead . . .

When Thou Walkest Through the Fire

Everett Smith

One fall morning some years ago, an automobile was seen moving along a highway in a northern section of Michigan. Soon it turned off into a side road that led through a large forest covered with pine and fir trees. A blond, blue-eyed young man sat behind the wheel casting glances at the fine forest of virgin timber.

The engine began to labor harder as he turned his car into the winding road that led up Lone Mountain. After reaching the two-thousand-foot level, where the road ended, Robert Mason left his car in the small parking space and began to climb the remaining distance. As he climbed, small stones were loosened by his feet and went cascading down the trail behind him. In twenty-five minutes, he had reached the top of the mountain, where a fire tower loomed 250 feet into the sky.

Bob had held the position of fire warden in that tower for two years. It was his duty to watch the surrounding territory and to report any fire or smoke that appeared in the forest.

He bounded up the twelve flights of stairs and took a quick look around. From the large window in the observation room, he could see for a distance of thirty miles on clear days. Large sections of timberland stretched out on every hand. To the south lay a village, and through the forest he could see small streams threading their way to the lake that lay farther to the west. There had been no rain in this part of the country for three weeks, and Bob was worried. The forest floor was dry as tinder; there was a blazing sun and a warm breeze.

In another section of the forest, about five miles to the north, two fishermen worked their way up a creek. As the sun approached the zenith, the younger of the two suggested that they stop and have lunch. As they were both hungry from their strenuous morning exercise, they agreed to stop under the large beech tree that stood around the next bend in the creek. Soon they had built a campfire, over which they prepared their dinner. Eager to get back to their fishing, they hurried away after the meal, leaving a few small embers of the fire still smoldering.

Bob Mason spent a good share of the morning looking through his high-powered glasses to make sure that a fire hidden somewhere did not get a start without his noticing it.

About one o'clock in the afternoon, he noticed a small spiral of smoke rising skyward in the north. When after a few minutes it seemed to increase, he decided that it might be a real fire and not just a camper's smoke. On his table was an Osborne fire finder, which in a few seconds told him the exact location of the smoke. Reaching for the phone, he called the nearest ranger station and asked the warden to send someone out to the location to investigate.

Soon a truck with two rangers in it roared out of the station. The U.S. Government has built good roads through the forests in all parts of the country to aid in fire protection. The rangers found the fire, and tried to stop it, but soon discovered that the few coals left by the fishermen had developed into a blaze too large for them to handle. They hurried back to the truck, and by means of a radio transmitter sent out a call for more men and equipment. This call brought hundreds of men from the surrounding territory to the scene of the fire.

Great clouds of smoke now billowed up into the sky. The men worked desperately, digging trenches and cutting away the brush in an effort to form a line where it would be possible to stop the onrushing destruction.

Bob Mason left the tower and drove down to the ranger station to see whether he could do anything to aid the firefighters. Since there was need for someone to drive an ambulance to bring out the burned or wounded men, Bob offered to help in that way.

As he approached the scene of disaster, he saw great tongues of flame leaping skyward. Whole sections of trees would burst into flames at the same instant. The roar of the fire sounded like the rumble of a thousand freight trains crossing steel trestles. He stopped and went around the side of the ambulance, lifted out the stretcher, and soon was busily engaged in carrying men to the nearest hospital, ten miles distant. The less seriously injured were treated at the temporary first-aid station set up near the fighting front.

The fire grew worse. Day after day, men came off the lines with their faces blackened, eyebrows burned off, and shirts hanging in shreds from blistered shoulders.

Near noon on the third day, a man came running up to Bob and asked him to come and help try to rescue his comrade, who was lying near the edge of the onrushing flames. A tree had fallen on him, crushing his leg. Carrying the stretcher, Bob followed his guide into the very thick of the smoke. They choked; their eyes smarted; the heat parched their throats. The injured man was lying on a bed of pine needles. As they carefully lifted him to the stretcher and started back to the ambulance, the fire grew fiercer and seemed to be burning on all sides. Soon they were surrounded with what seemed a solid wall of fire that offered no way of escape. In a very few moments, the main force of the tempest of flame would roar over the very ground where they stood.

The man with a broken leg gazed up at Bob and asked, "Won't you please pray?" Memories of his past quickly dashed through the young man's mind. He recalled his early boyhood and thought of his godly parents, of how they had taught him to pray and to love the Lord, of the day when he had left that home and struck out for himself. For a while he had held to his high principles, but gradually through the years of association with men of the world, he had forgotten God and had not prayed for fully five years. But right then and there, as he faced almost certain death, Bob Mason threw himself on his knees and sent up a petition for help to the Father above. Solemnly, he vowed that if the Lord spared his life, he would serve Him faithfully.

As he rose from his knees, it seemed that an audible voice said to him, *"Walk a little to your right."* Bob turned and asked which of his companions had spoken, but both denied that they had said a word. Soon the command came again. This time they obeyed, and after working their way through the smoke for about one hundred feet, they came upon a good-sized creek. Quickly they plunged in, waded to the center, and sat down in the water with only their faces exposed. Then they soaked the thick canvas stretcher and put it over their heads, thus forming a small pocket above the water. Almost immediately the flames roared above them, burning with intense heat. Several times they were obliged to hold their breath and duck under water while they soaked their stretcher shelter to keep it from bursting into flame. But finally the fire passed, and the three men could leave the creek.

On the bank once more, they thanked the Lord for His protecting hand, which had been placed over them in their hour of extreme need.

Bob sincerely believes that the voice that directed him to the creek was that of an angel sent in answer to his cry for help. That experience marked his conversion, and he never tires of witnessing for the Lord and telling of His mighty power.

Truly the day of miracles is not yet past. The divine promise still holds good: "Before they call, I will answer; and while they are yet speaking, I will hear" [Isaiah 65:24].

*A*gain and again, we discover in true miracle stories, God waits until His children pray the prayer of relinquishment. Though God is omnipotent, He absolutely refuses to invade our will. Only when we surrender our will to Him can He step in. This is why Catherine Marshall maintained that the prayer of relinquishment is the most powerful prayer a human being can pray.

Hearing about this book, this author (a cherished friend) rushed this story off to me. In her covering letter were these words: "I awoke this morning with a strong impression from the Lord to write one of my stories . . . for your compilation on miracles . . . and send it to you today!" Needless to say: it had *to* be included.

MY PRAYER OF RELINQUISHMENT

Teresa Sales

Prior to our retirement from nearly four decades of denominational work, we asked the Lord to help us find a small church without a resident pastor where we could continue to be of assistance. We had hinted to Him especially about one place in Colorado that we had always loved, but the Lord made it very clear this was not the one He had in mind when we were unable to afford even a very small house in that area.

At camp meeting the previous summer, a couple had approached us and asked us to consider moving to Paonia, a lovely small town in the mountains of western Colorado. The small church there shared a pastor, who lived about forty minutes away, with two other churches.

After visiting the area, falling in love with it, and praying earnestly, we felt that this was the way the Lord was leading us. We went back to Paonia in the fall and were even more convinced of God's leading when we discovered that some of the coal mines had shut down and houses were being sold at considerably less than their market value. We were able to find a lovely home on a mesa near the small church for about the price a vacant lot was selling for in the first place we had considered.

We sold our home in Alamosa to purchase the house in Paonia, spending our last seven months in the San Luis Valley in a tiny rented adobe during one of the worst winters ever recorded in the valley's history. The mercury hit forty-five below night after night, with daily highs in single digits! Still, we were excited about the proposition that when spring came we would be leaving full-time work and moving to the place the Lord had chosen for us to serve Him in retirement.

Our last Friday afternoon in Alamosa, our oldest daughter and her father went downtown to hunt behind businesses for more empty boxes. We laughed that this was always a big part of any move—we always miscalculated how many boxes we would need for our extensive library! When they came back, Beth was nursing a bad bruise from a fall she had taken while running down an alley, and her father was holding his side.

"I was reaching deep inside a dumpster for a box," he explained, "and hit my ribs on the sharp edge of the dumpster; it nearly knocked the wind out of me. That's going to be sore for quite a while, I'm afraid."

The next morning was as emotional as we had imagined it might be. My husband had written a farewell sermon that I knew would be hard for him to deliver—and it was. He also seemed very weary, but I attributed it to all the packing we had done during the week. After hugging all of our dear members at the final potluck, we took one last walk along the Rio Grande, and our oldest daughter and her husband returned to their home in Denver. My husband seemed very subdued; I thought it was because he was ending the happiest portion of his years of ministry.

After our Alamosa daughter and her husband went back to their new home, my husband said he thought he would have to lie down. I glanced over at his ashen face and said I thought a visit to the emergency room might be in order!

Things happened rapidly after that! The X-rays revealed that Don had actually broken some ribs when he hit the sharp edge of the dumpster. I was told that he was suffering from a high fever, and pneumonia was suspected—and shortly confirmed. He was transferred to a hospital room, and IVs were started.

Things worsened quickly, however. The fever did not break on Sunday, but instead escalated. A compassionate doctor, whom we had never met before, kept assuring me that the antibiotics would soon conquer the infection and my husband would be facing a slow, but sure, recovery.

I wanted to believe that this was just a minor bump in the path to a new phase of our service for the Lord. On each trip to the hospital, though, I saw him getting weaker and the nurses who were attending him getting more worried.

Monday morning I went to the hospital and prayed earnestly at the bed of my nonresponsive husband. One of the nurses stood close by me, her face showing her concern for both of us. "We're doing all we can to save him," she said.

"I know," I told her. "It's in the Lord's hands now." I said I'd be back in the afternoon and walked slowly down the hall to the elevator. The medical staff was doing all they could to save my husband; hundreds of people were praying for his life; we had a future planned to continue in a new area of service—what was going wrong?

"I don't understand this, Lord," I said, as I finished scrubbing the rental in preparation for the new occupants. "We've served You faithfully all these years; You've led us to another field of service in our retirement; what is happening here, and why?" The more I pleaded for my sweetheart of more than forty years, the less I felt the prayers were being heard.

I filled our car with last-minute debris and headed out of town to the city dump, totally disheartened. The recollection of my husband's still face on the hospital pillow was more than I could handle. Halfway to the dump, I pulled the car to the shoulder of the road and glanced at my watch. It was 2:00 P.M. I began sobbing, and then I prayed a prayer of relinquishment to the Lord.

"I'm sorry, Lord," I cried. "I've been giving You orders because I thought what I wanted was what You also planned for us. Please forgive me. I am willing now to accept whatever is

Your will for my husband and for me, even if I don't understand it." I sat in silence for some time, tears pouring down my face. Finally, a sense of peace came over me. Whatever happened, it would be God's will.

After leaving the landfill, I cleaned myself up and ran a couple of necessary errands before heading to the hospital. It was 4:00 P.M. when I walked down the hall to my husband's room.

My favorite nurse came running out of the room and greeted me with a big smile. "He's going to be all right!" she said. "He's very weak, but he's going to recover. His fever broke at two o'clock!"

The significance of the time did not escape me. The Lord had waited for me to quit giving Him orders, had waited for my surrender to His will, before answering my prayer. ❧

*M*iracles come in many forms. Ida Scudder was determined to return home to America—and stay there! No missionary life for her.

And the miracle? Just three knocks.

Coincidence—those three consecutive calls? You decide.

THE GIRL WHO CHANGED HER MIND

Margaret Eggleston

I want my mother! I want my own dear mother! It isn't fair to leave me here alone to go to school!" The girl cried as if her heart would break. "I shall never go to India to live. *Never! Never!*"

Young Ida Scudder belonged to a Reformed Church in America missionary family. Fifteen Scudders had dedicated their lives in service for India. Ida had lived there herself for many years, but when the family returned to the States on furlough, they left the teenage girl in Chicago with friends. In this way, she would be able to attend Northfield Seminary to further her education.

Ida pulled out a handkerchief and wiped her tear-streaked cheeks. *I know Mother is needed in India,* she reasoned. *She felt it was best for me to stay here alone for my education; but oh, how I want her! When I have children of my own, I won't go off and leave them.*

As time went by, Ida adjusted to her new life. She enjoyed her school and made many friends. Living away from her parents no longer seemed so difficult, and she began making plans for a secure future in America.

"What will you do when you graduate?" her friends often asked. "I'm not sure," was her reply. "Perhaps teach; maybe go into business."

"Won't you go back to India as a missionary?" they teased, knowing her strong feelings on the subject.

"Never! Mission life isn't for me! I plan to live in America. Fifteen good Scudders are enough to give to India. My work is here."

Then, just before graduation, Ida received a letter from her father. "Your mother is very ill," she read. "We need you here to care for her. Please come as soon as you can."

Ida immediately prepared to sail for India. If her mother needed her, of course she would go. It would be wonderful to see her family again. And she could always come back as soon as her mother recovered.

"I'll see you again soon," she waved to her friends as she left the school. "I won't be staying long."

The first few weeks of her stay in India were too busy for much else besides nursing her mother. But as soon as Mrs. Scudder began to feel better, discontent began rising in Ida's heart. In her imagination, she could see herself with the girls on the beautiful campus near the Connecticut River. What a far cry from the steam and squalor of India! She began making plans to return to America.

One night she sat writing to a friend in the

States. "Dear Annie," she wrote, "I am sitting in my room with your letter in front of me. It is late at night, and the compound is so quiet I can almost hear a lizard darting up the wall to catch a bug. My father is working in his bedroom-study next door, and my mother, I hope, is asleep. She is much better and should be quite well by the time my short term is finished. You say you wish you were a missionary like me. *Don't say that!* I'm not a missionary and never will be . . ."

Ida heard a discreet cough from the veranda outside. People were always coming, at any hour of the day or night, to ask her father for help. Picking up her lamp, she went to the door.

A dignified, somber young Indian stood there.

"What can I do for you?" the girl asked.

The man lifted trembling hands in a gesture of greeting. "I desperately need your help," he began in an unsteady voice. "My wife, a young girl of only fourteen, is dying in childbirth. She is such a lovely girl! I heard you had come from America, and I thought you might help her."

"Oh!" sympathized Ida. "I'm so sorry. But it's my father that you need. He's the doctor. Come, I'll take you to him." Before her eyes, the man seemed to change from a desperate young husband into an outraged, disdainful Brahman priest.

"What! Take a man into my house to care for my wife? No man other than those of her own family has ever looked upon her. You don't know what you say!"

"B-But," stammered Ida, "surely to save her life . . ."

"It is better that she should die," declared the young man. "You will not come?"

She shook her head. "It would do no good. I don't know anything." Ida watched the man turn and disappear into the darkness. *If only I had been ready,* she thought, *perhaps I could have saved her life.* She returned to her room and began writing furiously.

". . . and they're so young, Annie, not nearly as old as we are . . ." she continued, telling Annie all the reasons why she could never live in India as a missionary.

The sound of footsteps came again. Ida sprang to the door. Perhaps the young Brahman had changed his mind. But a different face appeared in the flickering lamplight.

"*Salaam,* madam. May Allah give you peace. If you would help . . ." The man's voice trailed off into the night.

"Of course," Ida replied without thinking. "What can I do for you?"

"It's my wife. She has had other children, but this time the little one does not come. There is no one to help her but an ignorant, untrained woman." The man moved closer. "I have heard there is a doctor here, recently come from America."

Ida looked closely at the man. He was a Muslim, and would not be bound by the Hindu laws. Surely her father could help this time. "Oh, yes!" she responded with enthusiasm. "My father can come right away."

"Madam," the voice was soft but firm, "you

do not understand. Only the men of her immediate family ever enter a Muslim woman's apartment. It is you, a woman, whose help I seek."

"But I can't help you. I'm not even a nurse. I'd be glad to help if I could."

"Then my wife must die," the man replied. "It is the will of Allah." He turned and was gone. Going straight back to her desk, Ida once again began writing.

"You see, Annie, why you wouldn't like being a missionary, especially in India. You'd simply hate it, and I ought to know. Believe me, I'm going to get back home just as quickly as I possibly can . . ."

And then the third call came. Ida moved once more to the door. She recognized the man as the father of one of the pupils at a school down the street. His wife was a lovely young woman with a shy smile and shining eyes.

"I have much trouble." The man lifted his hands in supplication. "I beg you, come to my house. My wife is sick, much sick." He threw himself on the veranda floor, his hands touching her feet. "I beg you to come. If not, my wife dies."

"But—it would do no good for me to come. I'm not a doctor. Let me call Father. If you'll just let him . . ." She knew it would do no good. The man lifted himself to his feet, outraged and bitter.

"Then you will not come?"

Ida slowly shook her head. "I'm sorry. I'd go if it would do any good. But it won't. Don't you understand?" Her voice rose a tone higher. "There's nothing—*nothing at all*—that I could do!"

All night the girl tossed and turned on her bed. *Father cannot help them because their religion will not allow it,* she thought. *Their need of a woman doctor is very great. If I were a doctor in America, life would be happy and clean. I do not want to live in India.*

Very early in the morning she sent a servant to inquire at the homes of the three women. "All are dead," he reported when he returned. "All are dead."

"Dead!" repeated the girl. "Three are dead! Three knocks at the door; three calls for help. Like Samuel, I believe I have been called of God."

The letter to Annie Hancock still lay on her desk. She picked it up and tore it into small pieces. With a determined stride, she went to her father's bedroom-study. "I'm going to America so I can study to be a doctor," she announced. "Then I can come back here and help the women of India."

In later years, Dr. Ida Scudder, head of the Mary Tabor Schell Hospital in Vellore, India, willingly took her place in the long line of Scudders who have served God and their fellow men and women there.

"God called me and I went," she told a friend. "My heavenly Father knows best where a life should be spent." ❧

*E*ven pastors have their down days; for Pastor Ken Gaub, this was one of them. He wondered, God, sometimes I wonder if You really know where I am! *Little did he know, but his cocoon of despondency was about to be shattered by the ringing of a pay phone.*

Not often, in this hectic troubled life that we live, are we given an experience that confirms for us, once and for all, that God really exists. This is just such a story.

GOD'S GOT YOUR NUMBER!

Ken Gaub

God, sometimes I wonder if You really know where I am! I mused to myself. A melancholy cloud of self-pity enshrouded my mind as I tried to concentrate on driving.

God, even a preacher needs for You to let him know once in a while that You are aware of him, I mentally implored.

"Hey, Dad. Let's get some pizza." The voice of my son, Dan, snapped me out of my self-induced cocoon of despondency. The voices of my wife, Barbara, and daughter, Becki, chimed in agreement with Dan. It had been a long day, and it was way past time to eat.

"OK," I yelled back. Exiting from I-75 we turned onto Route 741 just south of Dayton, Ohio. Bright colorful signs advertising a wide variety of fast-food restaurants welcomed us.

Before I had fully parked, the kids were clamoring to get out. Barbara stepped to the bottom stair of our "home on wheels" and stopped. "Aren't you coming, Ken?" she quizzed.

"Naw, I'm not really hungry," I replied. "You just go ahead with the kids. I need to stretch out and unwind a bit."

I stepped outside. Noticing a Dairy Queen down the street, I thought, *I really am thirsty.*

After purchasing a soft drink, I strolled slowly back, all the while musing about my feelings of God's apathy toward me. The sudden ringing of a telephone somewhere up the street jarred me out of my doldrums. It was coming from a phone booth at the service station on the corner.

I drew near and paused. I looked around to see if anyone was going to answer. The service station attendant seemed oblivious to the incessant ringing of the nearby phone.

I started to walk on past, but curiosity overcame my indifference. I stepped inside the booth and picked up the phone. "Hello," I said casually.

The operator intoned nasally, "Long-distance call for Ken Gaub."

My eyes widened and I almost choked on a chunk of ice from my drink. Swallowing hard, I replied in astonishment, "You're crazy!" Realizing my rude remark, I added, "This can't be! I was just walking down the street, not bothering anyone, and the phone was just ringing . . ."

The operator ignored my crude explanation and asked once more, "Is Ken Gaub there? I have a long-distance call for him."

Searching for a possible explanation, I suddenly had the answer: *I know what this is! I'm on* Candid Camera*!*

I reached up and tried to smooth my hair. I wanted to look my best for all those millions of television viewers watching me. I stepped outside the phone booth looking quickly in every direction. I nearly broke the telephone cord as I stretched it to its limit. I couldn't find a camera anywhere! Impatiently, the operator interrupted again.

"I have a long-distance call for Ken Gaub. Is he there?"

Flustered, I half-laughingly replied, "As far as I know at this point, I am."

To avoid any further disasters, I set my drink down as I heard another voice interject, "Yes, that's him, operator. I believe that's him!"

I listened dumbfounded to a strange voice identify herself. The caller blurted, "Ken Gaub, I'm Millie from Harrisburg, Pennsylvania. You don't know me, but I'm desperate. Please help me."

She began weeping. I waited until she had regained control of herself. She continued, "I'm about to commit suicide. I just finished writing a note and while writing it, I began to pray. I told God I really didn't want to do this. While I was writing this note, I suddenly remembered seeing you on television in Harrisburg. I thought if I could just talk to you, you could help me. I knew that was impossible because I didn't know how to reach you and I didn't know anyone who could help me find you. While I was writing, numbers began to come to my mind and I wrote them down."

While still listening, I began to pray silently for wisdom to help her.

She continued, "I looked at the numbers and thought, *Wouldn't it be wonderful if I had a miracle from God and He has given me Ken's phone number?* I decided to try calling it. I figured it was worth the chance. It really was. I can't believe I'm talking to you. Are you in your office?"

I replied, "Lady, my office is in Yakima, Washington."

A little surprised, she asked, "Oh, really? Then where are you?"

"Ma'am, you won't believe this, but I'm in a phone booth in Dayton, Ohio!"

Knowing this encounter could have been arranged only by God, I began to counsel seriously with the woman. She told me of her despair and frustration. In a matter of moments, she prayed the sinner's prayer and met the only Person who could lead her out of her situation into a new life—Jesus Christ.

I walked away from that telephone booth with an electrifying sense of our heavenly Father's concern for each of His children. *With all the millions of phones and innumerable combinations of numbers, only an all-knowing God could have caused that woman to call that number in that phone booth at that moment in time.*

Nearly bursting with exhilaration, I bounded up the steps into the bus. I wondered if my family would believe my story.

"Barb, you won't believe this! *God knows where I am!*" ❦

EPILOGUE

I not only had no intention of including the following story in this collection—I hadn't even written it—but because of an extraordinary sequence of events sometime after this manuscript had been turned in and accepted, I became convicted that God willed it to be written down so that it could serve as the epilogue for this collection.

Here is what triggered it:

Jerry D. Thomas (my chief editor at Pacific Press®) wrote to me, relaying a request from the editorial team that I expand each story's introduction so that it would be clearer to the readers what my personal reasons were for including it.

At a May 2014 alumni weekend at my undergraduate alma mater, Pacific Union College in California's Napa Valley, along with four other honored alumni, we were each asked to distill for the audience the most significant lessons, events, or wisdom accumulated during our lifetimes. After I'd dutifully done my best to comply, the moderator, Dr. Bruce Anderson (a long ago classmate and trusted friend), surprised me by asking if I'd mind sharing the story of a life-changing airplane flight. I did so, and it so moved the audience that afterward I couldn't get the story out of my head.

On the way back to Colorado in an Amtrak observation car, as we were crossing the snow-capped Sierra Nevada, I got into a discussion with a sizable group of young people about their goals in life. It took several hours before the impromptu discussion wound down. One of the students told me later, "I got on this train because I was hoping to find answers to questions about life."

Many years before this train experience, the untimely death of the primary mentor of my lifetime, Dr. Walter Utt of Pacific Union College, changed my life. In gratitude to him, I vowed to make mentoring the number one priority for the rest of my life. From that day to this, I have done my best to keep that vow.

Thus, it was that, upon my return, as I expanded my story introductions, I was strongly convicted that I should write down the story of that never-to-be-forgotten flight and add it to the book as the epilogue.

MIRACLE IN THE SKY

Joseph Leininger Wheeler

Have you ever wondered, Is God real? Or might God be merely a construct created for church leaders who have ulterior motives for instituting and maintaining their sects and religions? *Chances are, every one of us has, at one time or another, wondered; though even to do so,* *especially for a person who was born into a Christian home, even to wonder about such a thing seems tantamount to blasphemy.*

Yet, even I must admit that I have wondered. But not anymore—and herein lies this story.

A number of years ago, shortly after we had moved from Maryland to Colorado, I was sitting in the Baltimore-Washington International Airport waiting area, listening for the announcement that boarding was beginning for my flight to Denver. As I have done for many years, when I am alone, I prayed that God would select the person who would sit next to me; that it would be either someone who would share something with me I needed to know or someone who God willed should talk with me.

After I did so, I looked around the waiting room to see who appeared to be flying solo like me. Would it be the distinguished man with a carefully manicured goatee? The grandmotherly woman with laugh lines etched on her face? The businessman rummaging around in his briefcase? The beautiful young woman who attracted so much attention? The scruffy-looking man who seemed ill at ease? Or might it be one of the many couples traveling together or a mother with her child? Since the plane was full, I knew *someone* would have to settle for the middle seat next to me.

Finally, the boarding process began. I shoved my suitcase into the overhead compartment, took my seat, and watched the people streaming down the aisle. But no one took that middle seat. There were very few open seats left when the very last person I wanted to be stuck next to for more than three hours walked toward me! You know the type: the person who talks five times as loud as anyone else, on his cell phone, showing *everyone* how important he is by the one-sided conversation that is impossible not to hear!

As he neared me, I muttered to the good

Lord, "Please, not him; don't stick me with him—the most obnoxious person in the entire terminal!"

But my pleading with God was to no avail. As the man neared me, he didn't even ask if he could sit next to me, but rather jabbed his finger in the general direction of that middle seat. I stood up, he sat down, and before the plane had even left the ground, he had begun his *very loud* rant. He told me, *us,* how important he was, how misunderstood he was, how his first wife had left him and his second, and now his third was threatening to leave him, how his children did not respect him as they ought to—in fact, *hated* him, how the whole world would have to eat crow after he wrote the hit song that would make him world famous. Half an hour later, he paused to take a breath.

I shifted my body toward the aisle in hopes that the man next to me would get the hint. Seething, I all but snarled as I muttered, "Lord, You've let me down big time!" Over the years, I've developed a relationship with God in which my communication with Him occurs throughout the day. I never hang up the phone, so the line remains open.

Not surprisingly, God countered, *What was that prayer you prayed?*

I answered, "But Lord, I've *listened* to him all through the nonstop harangue. What more could You expect out of me?"

Again, *What was that prayer you prayed?*

This time, I was angry, for I didn't want to hear one more word out of my seatmate. And I told God so.

Again, God spoke—and this time with no-nonsense authority: *What was that prayer you prayed?*

I finally gave up. I unbuckled my seat belt, stood up, rummaged around in my briefcase, took out a book, closed the case, and sat down. Somewhat sheepishly, I turned to the man next to me, cleared my throat, and said, "This is my new book. I thought you might be interested in it."

Without a word, he reached for it, opened it up, turned to the introduction, and began to read. I surreptitiously watched. The book was *Dad in My Heart* (a collection of fatherhood stories, copublished by Focus on the Family and Tyndale House; later published in hardback as *Heart to Heart Stories for Dads*). I inwardly shuddered as I looked across at the title to the introduction: "Fathers on Castors: The Disappearing Father in America Today." I'd forgotten about that introduction when I handed the book to him. For if there were ever a poster child for that title, it was the man sitting next to me! I waited for the explosion. And waited. And waited.

Slowly, he continued to read. He read on and on. He finished the introduction and turned to the first story, Joan Marie Cook's "The Yellow Shirt," and the second, Hattie H. Carpenter's "As a Grain of Mustard Seed." A half hour had passed without one solitary word being spoken.

He now stared glassy-eyed, seeing but not seeing, toward the front of the plane, almost as though he was in a trance.

Then he turned to me and said, in a normal voice, "I have no business being on this plane today. There is no earthly reason why I should be on this plane. But a *Voice* kept telling me, 'Buy a ticket to Denver and get on the plane!' " Then, jabbing his finger at me once more, he said, *"God put you on this plane!"*

My blood froze. *Here I was doing a pouty Jonah act!* I've never felt more ashamed in my entire life.

He continued, "How can I get this book?"

That was easy to do. I asked him to hand me the book, personally inscribed it to him, then handed it back to him.

Then, in a soft voice, he asked me about *many* things, and I did my best to answer them.

Just before the plane began its descent to Denver, I took his hand and prayed for him.

But before we got up to disembark, he said one more thing, "You know what I'm going to do?"

"No."

"I'm going to rent a car in the terminal, drive up into the high country, read your book, and learn how to be a dad."

And then we parted.

I've never heard from him since. But as for me, that was the defining moment in my lifetime, for finally I knew, with absolute certainty, that *God is real, He condescends to be my Partner in this ministry of stories, and never again can I doubt Him, for, moment by moment, He remains at my side.* ❧

ACKNOWLEDGMENTS

Introduction: "Is There a Difference Between Miracle Stories and Coincidence Stories?" by Joseph Leininger Wheeler. Copyright © 2014. Printed by permission of the author.

"The Lord Spoke to Me," by Dr. James Dobson. Published in Dobson's book, *Your Legacy* (New York: Faith Words / Hachette Book Group, 2014). Reprinted by permission of the author.

SECTION ONE

"The Boy in the Well," by Mrs. Sam Woodson. If anyone can provide information about the author, the author's next of kin, or the first publication of this story, please relay to Joe Wheeler (P.O. Box 1246, Conifer, CO 80433).

"Prayer Heard and Answered," by author unknown. Published in *The Youth's Instructor*, April 13, 1920. Reprinted by permission of Review and Herald® Publishing Association, Hagerstown, MD 21740.

"The Voice in the Tiger Jungle," by Jacob Chamberlain. Published in W. A. Spicer's book *The Hand That Intervenes* (Washington, D.C.: Review and Herald® Publishing Association, 1918). Original text owned by Joe Wheeler.

"The Unseen Hand," by Jean Crager. Published in *The Youth's Instructor*, October 13, 1931. Reprinted by permission of Review and Herald® Publishing Association, Hagerstown, MD 21740. If anyone can provide information about the author or the author's next of kin, please relay to Joe Wheeler (P.O. Box 1246, Conifer, CO 80433).

"The Expunged Sermon," by John F. Fletcher. Published in W. A. Spicer's book *The Hand That Intervenes* (Washington, D.C.: Review and Herald® Publishing Association, 1918). Original text owned by Joe Wheeler.

"Poisoned in Tibet," by William Carey. Published in W. A. Spicer's book *The Hand That Intervenes* (Washington, D.C.: Review and Herald® Publishing Association, 1918). Original text owned by Joe Wheeler.

"A Box for Su Ling," by Theresa Worman. Taken with permission of Moody Publishers from *My Favorite Christmas Stories* by Theresa Worman © 1965.

"A Life-Changing Day on Humboldt Bay," by Kirby Palmer, Connie Palmer Wheeler, and Marla Palmer Marsh. Copyright © 2014. Printed by permission of the authors.

SECTION TWO

"His Daily Bread," by Mrs. Howard Taylor. Published in W. A. Spicer's book *The Hand That Intervenes* (Washington, D.C.: Review and Herald® Publishing Association, 1918). Original text owned by Joe Wheeler.

"A Raven the Messenger," by S. W. Duffield. Published in W. A. Spicer's book *The Hand That Intervenes* (Washington, D.C.: Review and Herald® Publishing Association, 1918). Original text owned by Joe Wheeler.

"Miracle in the Landhouse" (A Narrative of Reformation Times) published in W. A. Spicer's book *The Hand That Intervenes* (Washington, D.C.: Review and Herald® Publishing Association, 1918). Original text owned by Joe Wheeler.

"Why the Horse Balked," retold by H. W. Hastings. Published in W. A. Spicer's book *The Hand That Intervenes* (Washington, D.C.: Review and Herald® Publishing Association, 1918). Original text owned by Joe Wheeler.

"Saved by a Spider's Web," by Baxendale. Published in W. A. Spicer's book *The Hand That Intervenes* (Washington, D.C.: Review and Herald® Publishing Association, 1918). Original text owned by Joe Wheeler.

SECTION THREE

"Snatched From the Green River," by Byron Palmer. Copyright © 2014. Printed by permission of the author.

"A Rescue at Sea," by Helen A. Steinhauer. Published in W. A. Spicer's book *The Hand That Intervenes* (Washington, D.C.: Review and Herald® Publishing Association, 1918). Original text owned by Joe Wheeler.

"Oranges From Heaven," by Miriam Kershaw. Published in *The Youth's Instructor,* January 15, 1918. Reprinted by permission of Review and Herald® Publishing Association, Hagerstown, MD 21740.

"Adrift in the Heavens," by Myrtle Cossentine. Published in *The Youth's Instructor,* February 8, 1934. Reprinted by permission of Review and Herald® Publishing Association, Hagerstown, MD 21740. If anyone can provide information about the author or the author's next of kin, please relay to Joe Wheeler (P.O. Box 1246, Conifer, CO 80433).

"The Plane Engine That Wouldn't Start," by Gary Marsh. Copyright © 2014. Printed by permission of the author.

"Jungle Landing," by George Alden

Thompson. Published in *The Youth's Instructor,* April 28, 1953. Reprinted by Review and Herald® Publishing Association, Hagerstown, MD 21740. If anyone can provide information about the author or the author's next of kin, please relay to Joe Wheeler (P.O. Box 1246, Conifer, CO 80433).

"Miracle in Magdeburg," by Paul K. Freiwirth. Published in *The Youth's Instructor,* May 1, 1951. Reprinted by Review and Herald® Publishing Association, Hagerstown, MD 21740. If anyone can provide information about the author or the author's next of kin, please relay to Joe Wheeler (P.O. Box 1246, Conifer, CO 80433).

"Revolution!" by Joseph Leininger Wheeler. Copyright © 2014. Printed by permission of the author.

SECTION FOUR

"An Angry Mob Held Powerless," by Adam Clarke. Published in W. A. Spicer's book *The Hand That Intervenes* (Washington, D.C.: Review and Herald® Publishing Association, 1918). Original text owned by Joe Wheeler.

"How Wang Was Called Into the Light," by Hudson Taylor. Published in W. A. Spicer's book *The Hand That Intervenes* (Washington, D.C.: Review and Herald® Publishing Association, 1918). Original text owned by Joe Wheeler.

"The Missionary Digs a Well," by John G. Paton. Published in *The Youth's Instructor,* August 14, 1928. Reprinted by permission of Review and Herald® Publishing Association, Hagerstown, MD 21740.

"Protected," by Mary Markham. Published in *The Youth's Instructor,* April 13, 1937. Reprinted by permission of Review and Herald® Publishing Association, Hagerstown, MD 21740. If anyone can provide information about the author or the author's next of kin, please relay to Joe Wheeler (P.O. Box 1246, Conifer, CO 80433).

"The Shadow," by Jean Wingate. Published in *The Youth's Instructor,* September 16, 1930. Reprinted by permission of Review and Herald® Publishing Association, Hagerstown, MD 21740. If anyone can provide information about the author or the author's next of kin, please relay to Joe Wheeler (P.O. Box 1246, Conifer, CO 80433).

"Nondis the Leper," by Marjorie Lewis Lloyd. Published in Marjorie Lewis Lloyd's book *It Must Have Been an Angel,* 1978. Reprinted by permission of Pacific Press® Publishing Association, Nampa, ID 83687. If anyone can provide information about the author, the author's next of kin, or the first publication of this story, please relay to Joe Wheeler (P.O. Box 1246, Conifer, CO 80433).

"Another Chance," by Dawn Boylan.

Published in *Insight,* June 15, 1991. Reprinted by permission of Review and Herald® Publishing Association, Hagerstown, MD 21740. If anyone can provide information about the author, please relay to Joe Wheeler (P.O. Box 1246, Conifer, CO 80433).

"The Lighted Path," by Mrs. R. B. Sheffer. Published in *The Youth's Instructor,* November 5, 1946. Reprinted by permission of Review and Herald® Publishing Association, Hagerstown, MD 21740. If anyone can provide information about the author or the author's next of kin, please relay to Joe Wheeler (P.O. Box 1246, Conifer, CO 80433).

SECTION FIVE

"He Shall Give His Angels Charge," by Leta Walker. Published in *The Youth's Instructor,* June 11, 1946. Reprinted by permission of Review and Herald® Publishing Association, Hagerstown, MD 21740. If anyone can provide information about the author or the author's next of kin, please relay to Joe Wheeler (P.O. Box 1246, Conifer, CO 80433).

"Danger in the Dark," by Louis W. Pettis. Published in *The Youth's Instructor,* August 9, 1966. Reprinted by permission of Review and Herald® Publishing Association, Hagerstown, MD 21740. If anyone can provide information about the author or the author's next of kin, please relay to Joe Wheeler (P.O. Box 1246, Conifer, CO 80433).

"Angels in the Fog," by Lois Foreman. Published in *The Youth's Instructor,* June 26, 1945. Reprinted by permission of Review and Herald® Publishing Association, Hagerstown, MD 21740. If anyone can provide information about the author or the author's next of kin, please relay to Joe Wheeler (P.O. Box 1246, Conifer, CO 80433).

"Miracle on Highway 88," by Steve Hamilton. Copyright © 2010. Printed by permission of the author.

"When Thou Walkest Through the Fire," by Everett Smith. Published in *The Youth's Instructor,* October 27, 1942. Reprinted by permission of Review and Herald® Publishing Association, Hagerstown, MD 21740. If anyone can provide information about the author or the author's next of kin, please relay to Joe Wheeler (P.O. Box 1246, Conifer, CO 80433).

"My Prayer of Relinquishment," by Teresa Sales. Copyright © 2013. Printed by permission of the author.

"The Girl Who Changed Her Mind," by Margaret Eggleston. Published in Eggleston's book *Forty Missionary Stories* (New York: Harper & Brothers, 1934). If anyone knows the whereabouts of the author's next of kin, please relay to Joe Wheeler (P.O. Box 1246, Conifer, CO 80433).

EPILOGUE